Newton Heath

ENGINES AT WORK

1948-1968

Long-standing Newton Heath Stanier Jubilee 4-6-0 No 45661 *Vernon* passes Bury Gas Works Sidings on Easter Monday morning at 10.55am with a Rochdale to Blackpool ADEX. **15TH APRIL 1963** ● **E.F. BENTLEY**

To Neville from Paul

PAUL SHACKCLOTH

Newton Heath
ENGINES AT WORK
1948-1968

First published 2006

ISBN 0 9543128 3 X

Published by Steam Image, PO Box 90, Cheadle Hulme, Cheshire SK8 6WZ & printed by Deanprint Ltd, Stockport, Cheshire SK3 0PR.

FOREWORD

At the beginning of 1948, the majority of railways in Great Britain lost their separate identities and merged to become a national concern. As a consequence, British Railways inherited just over 20,000 steam locomotives housed in excess of 300 engine sheds built in many shapes and sizes.

One of the largest of these was Newton Heath, situated in the north east suburbs of Manchester and home to 172 engines at Nationalisation. This total was represented by 26 different classes which reflected the great diversity of duties carried out at the depot. The only notable absentees were the Class 8 passenger locos, the 'Princess Royals' and the 'Duchesses', as local clearance restrictions precluded their allocation.

Similar large establishments could be found at Stratford (London) - by far the biggest of them all, Carlisle (Kingmoor), Edge Hill (Liverpool) and Polmadie (Glasgow). Otherwise the principal depots tended to be either passenger or freight orientated - such was the situation at Bristol (Bath Road and St. Philips Marsh), Crewe (North and South), Hull (Botanic Gardens and Dairycoates) and London (Camden and Willesden - Kentish Town and Cricklewood) to name but a few.

Newton Heath was erected in 1876, replacing premises at Miles Platting which had become woefully inadequate. The 24 road through running shed, capable of housing 180 locomotives under cover, was easily the largest of the 32 depots within the L&Y system and was coded No 1. It had 100 engines on its books in 1876 but by 1922 this had risen to 232. Reorganisation by the LMS resulted in a change of shed code to 26A which it retained until September 1963. During the final years of steam, the depot suffered the ignominy of being placed under Longsight's control and a new batch of 9D shedplates were cast. The code had been Buxton's for many years but this depot, in turn, was further downgraded to 9L during its final years.

It was widely accepted that a Newton Heath engineman's route knowledge was second to none, a claim that seems justified when one considers the range of locations within this book, notwithstanding the fact that some engines were borrowed on occasion by other depots. A few of the older, usually smaller locos which barely survived Nationalisation have proved elusive in my quest to track down sufficient pictures of them at work. Also camera-shy was the only ex-LNER representative, B1 No 61326 during its short stay in the summer of 1950 - but I have included a shot in its Gorton days which I trust is acceptable. Similarly I have also included photos of the ex-GC 'Directors', Nos 62662/4 which worked out of the shed prior to a railtour. Naturally, the Jubilees feature prominently and the vast majority appear in alphabetical order by name. They were the depot's flagship engines but the popular and numerous Class Fives are also heavily represented.

This collection of photographs, arranged in class order within the BR renumbering scheme, has been drawn from a great number of sources to whom I offer both individuals and societies my heartfelt thanks. The criteria was that all locos had to be allocated at the time of the photograph and if any were in doubt, they were discarded. As is often the case, there are a few anonymous shots which can only be credited to the collector. If any have inadvertently slipped the net, please accept my apologies.

ACKNOWLEDGEMENTS

A historical examination of Newton Heath Motive Power Depot, its earlier locomotives and workings, buildings, staff and facilities etc. from inception through to the present day is beyond the scope of this work, but will hopefully form the subject of a further volume.

I am indeed fortunate in being able to select from the collections of Peter Fitton, Brian Green and Richard Greenwood, all of whom are highly respected photographers and whose work forms the backbone of the book. I am also indebted to a great many others, too numerous to mention individually, who have provided material for the remainder. Photographs credited to Kenneth Field, Tom Lewis, Eric Bentley and Jim Davenport appear courtesy of Rail Archive Stephenson, Ray Hinton and the MLS, Jean Bentley and Brian Green respectively.

Many other individuals have contributed in one way or another and special thanks must go to Fred Consterdine, Richard Cort, Bernard Crick, Alan Gilbert, John Hartshorne, Paul Jordan, Peter Michie, Trevor Moseley, Ken Royle, Allan Sommerfield and members of the Lancashire and Yorkshire and Manchester Locomotive Societies.

David Young, whose enthusiasm and diligence knows no bounds and Arthur Haynes continue to support and encourage in every conceivable way. Lastly, the Shackcloth family are now resigned to the fact that the writing of books about steam is a time-consuming, solitary affair. One day I must attempt to redress the balance.

NOVEMBER 2006 ● PAUL SHACKCLOTH

DEDICATION

I wish to dedicate this book to Gordon Coltas, an eminent photographer known by many who unfortunately passed away during the preparation of this book. Deteriorating health restricted his activities in latter years but I spent many happy hours in his company reminiscing and discussing all matters 'railway' and in particular the printing of photographs - a favourite pastime for both of us. I was more than happy to 'muck in' when he eventually requested assistance, but - naturally, it was a source of intense frustration that he was no longer able to print. His advice and encouragement will always remain precious. Gordon had been a prime mover with my first book 'Stockport in the Days of Steam', but once told me that he had a 'soft spot' for Newton Heath. This book therefore forms a fitting tribute.

In addition, I wish to couple this dedication to the many Newton Heath enginemen and staff, both past and present who served during the days of steam.

THE FOWLER 2-6-2 TANKS

The Blackpool Illuminations period in late Autumn resulted in the provision of many extras from towns within both Lancashire and Yorkshire and brought a late influx of motive power variety to the coast after the summer season. A typical Saturday evening excursion originating from Failsworth has been piloted around the Oldham Loop by Fowler 2-6-2T No **40015**. The train, made up of non-corridor stock, has arrived in Rochdale Station where No 40015 has already detached. The headlamps and reporting number have been transferred to the train engine, Crab 2-6-0 No **42728** - which will proceed via Bury Knowsley Street, Bolton and Preston. Meanwhile the 'breadvan' will return light engine to Newton Heath shed. Occupying one of the south west bays is a Cravens built DMU awaiting departure with a local service. If the two trainspotters on the Down platform are local lads, it's doubtful whether either engine would represent a 'cop' as both were relatively common sights here.   **10TH OCTOBER 1959** ● **R.S. GREENWOOD**

A representative of the class could often be found pottering about Victoria Station. 2-6-2T No **40014** is engaged on Bays Pilot duty, a turn also referred to as 'Turntable Pilot' and is standing almost within the shadow of Cheetham Hill Road bridge. A facility just out of view offered a quick turn round for engines handling the intensive local commuter services. The signalbox was similarly named and controlled all movements within the bay platforms (Nos 1 - 10). Many bus services crossed the bridge and the parapets, which were infuriatingly high, restricted any possible view from the upper decks - much to the consternation of the author and other fellow enthusiasts.

c.1955 ● **R.K. BLENCOWE COLLECTION**

A short ballast train passes Oldham Lees Sidings on a sunny morning behind 2-6-2T No **40063.** The engine's tank and cab sides are remarkably clean, revealing the fully lined out livery and the older 'ferret and dartboard' totem carried from the onset of Nationalisation. Immediately behind the loco is a lightly loaded bogie bolster wagon carrying rail sections, above which can be glimpsed another clean Fowler loco, in this case 0-8-0 No **49668** from nearby Lees (Oldham) MPD.

c.1956 ● J. DAVENPORT

Trundling through Castleton is Fowler 2-6-2T No **40015.** The loco is returning light engine to its home depot, having piloted a midday excursion to Blackpool around the Oldham Loop as far as Rochdale. It was similarly engaged later in the day with another train bound for the Fylde coast *(see previous page)* - not an unusual occurrence on busy days.

10TH OCTOBER 1959 ● R.S. GREENWOOD

As a rule, Newton Heath's 'breadvans' were only deployed on passenger duty when a tank engine of the Fairburn, Stanier or Standard variety was unavailable - such was their unpopularity with enginemen - a fact that 'authority' was well aware of. Fowler 2-6-2T No **40014** has been rostered for an outing around the Oldham Loop and is getting away from Royton Junction's Platform 1 with a stopping train to Manchester Victoria. The leading carriage is of interest, being of L&Y origin, as is the rather lofty 38 lever signalbox. The 1 1/2 mile Royton Branch, served by Platforms 3 and 4, is clearly visible trailing in from the left. **30TH JUNE 1956** ● **J. DAVENPORT**

Carriage Pilot duties were considered to be within their capabilities, though, and a loco was often rostered for work at Lightbowne Sidings - situated directly opposite Newton Heath MPD on the Down side of the main line. Fowler 2-6-2T No **40062** stands near the throat of the extensive site performing such a duty. Note the grounded vintage carriages acting as mess vans, behind which are a number of rakes of non-corridor excursion stock used for trains originating on the Central Division. **15TH APRIL 1954 ● H.C. CASSERLEY**

Another member on similar duties is 2-6-2T No **40013**. The location is a point midway between Red Bank and Cheetham Hill Carriage Sidings, situated on the South side of the loop line from Manchester Victoria East Junction to Thorpes Bridge Junction. A veritable hive of local industry in the Collyhurst area is still evident in the Irk Valley and just visible beneath the arm of the starting signal are railings protecting the 99 'Barneys Steps'. These were a local landmark offering pedestrian access from Collyhurst Road to North Street brickworks via an impressive four arched footbridge which straddled the sidings and main running lines. This early afternoon scene has been caught from a passing train, the 12.55pm ex Leeds, 1.15pm ex Bradford to Liverpool Exchange hauled by Bank Hall Caprotti Class Five No 44744. **10TH OCTOBER 1959 ● R.S. GREENWOOD**

The Salford Hundred Rail Tour offered a rare opportunity for one of the last survivors of the class, Fowler 2-6-2T No **40063,** to operate over local lines. It was deemed surplus to requirements in August 1960 and moved to Bolton MPD with other members of the class, Nos 40013 and 40062 for storage, prior to being broken up at nearby Horwich Works. No 40063, however, was utilised in traffic - appearing on the Moses Gate Pilot duty a number of times. It then languished in a 'stored but serviceable' condition at the rear of the depot for a number of months before the *Roch Valley Railway Society* approached the authorities with regards to its availability. This proved positive and although BR stated that although no additional manpower was available to improve its external appearance, members would be allowed access beforehand for a quick 'wash and brush up'.

◄ **40063 is caught trailing the train** and is going away from the camera, having just passed through the short Whitworth Road tunnel between Rochdale and Facit. Ex L&Y 'A' Class No 52523, involved in this part of the itinerary, heads the rail tour.

28TH JULY 1962 ● R.S. GREENWOOD

The Roch Valley Railway Society was formed in 1959 by a small band of enthusiasts in Rochdale and district. Having successfully organised the 'Central Lancashire Rail Tour' which involved Radial Tank No 50850 on 17th September 1960, nearly two years elapsed before their second effort. The 'Salford Hundred Rail Tour' again traversed miles of little used track in the Greater Manchester area. The full itinerary was as follows: Manchester Piccadilly - Park - Ashton Oldham Road - Oldham Clegg Street - Royton Junction - Rochdale - Facit - Rochdale - Castleton - Heap Bridge - Bury Knowsley Street - Tottington - Tottington Junction - Stubbins Junction - Bacup - Bury Bolton Street - Bradley Fold Junction - Radcliffe Central - Cheetham Hill Junction - Manchester Victoria. Ex L&Y 'A' Class No 52523 assisted on the Facit, Heap Bridge, Tottington and Bacup branches, taking over single handed from Bacup.

Leaving Tottington on the former Holcombe Brook branch, No **40063** working bunker first, crosses South Royds Street, having passed the Hargreaves and Jennings factory on the left. St. Annes cricket ground and Kirklees Street bridge (adjacent to Station) are to the right. A few enthusiasts have heads out of windows, the nearest sporting a trilby. Progress must have been slow! ►

28TH JULY 1962 ● E.F. BENTLEY

◄ **Middleton Station,** terminus of the short branch from Middleton Junction Station, is the setting for Fowler 2-6-2T No **40015** which has arrived on the 5.12pm from Manchester Victoria. A similar view - the previous frame on eminent photographer Henry Casserley's filmstrip that day, appeared in an earlier volume *Manchester in the Days of Steam.* The loco will shortly reverse the stock out of the arrival platform and run round its train prior to propelling the carriages back into the Up platform where a few mailbags on trolleys await loading - but precious few passengers. A familiar face is visible on an advertising billboard - Dennis Compton - one of a small number of sportsmen who represented his country at both Association Football and Cricket and was long associated with Brylcreem. He played for Arsenal and Middlesex respectively.

11TH JUNE 1951 ● H.C. CASSERLEY

THE FAIRBURN 2-6-4 TANKS

One of Newton Heath's last regular tank-hauled duties was the 5.47pm workmen's train from Horwich to Manchester Victoria. Fairburn 2-6-4T No **42115** gets away on time with its train of non-corridor stock and is passing under the bridge carrying Chorley New Road alongside the small 44 lever ex L&Y signalbox. Passenger services were withdrawn a week later, having survived this long supposedly for the benefit of railway employees at the works. **20TH SEPTEMBER 1965 ● P. FITTON**

The crew of Fairburn 2-6-4T No 42079 are no doubt thankful for clear signals as the 4.20pm Manchester Victoria to Colne approaches Ringley Road (Radcliffe) up the 1 in 79 incline. Fresh ballast and a recently painted sighting board are evident but this was a tightly timed train. After calling at Salford and travelling by way of Clifton Junction, one minute only (4.44pm - 4.45pm) was allowed for the second stop at Bury Bolton Street and Colne was reached at 5.42pm. **19TH APRIL 1963 ● E.F. BENTLEY**

A 26A member showing Class A headlamps makes haste towards Blackrod with what one assumes to be an express working making for the Fylde coast. Fast running may also be the possible reason for the pasted Central Division Reporting Number coming adrift from its backboard - thus rendering its identification anonymous. In addition - the train, consisting of a smart set of blood and custard stock, is of five carriages only and may well be privately chartered. The light load is certainly well within the capabilities of Fairburn 2-6-4T No **42279**.

c.1956 ● J. DAVENPORT

The 9.50am Bolton to Rochdale train was always composed of just two coaches detached from the 8.20am Blackpool Central to Manchester Victoria. They were a First Open and a Second Brake Open so that first class accommodation outnumbered that of the second class! Historically, it provided a facility for the cotton mill owners to commute from the Fylde to Radcliffe, Bury, Heywood and Rochdale. The morning sun catches Fairburn 2-6-4T No **42696** getting smartly away from Burnden Junction, Bolton. **28TH SEPTEMBER 1960 ● D. HAMPSON**

As a result of the official closure of Lees (Oldham) MPD on Monday, 13th April 1964, Newton Heath received an influx of nine locos including a pair of Fairburn 2-6-4T's, Nos **42079** and 42115. The remainder of the allocation, four Ivatt 2-6-0s, went to Springs Branch, Wigan. Coming off shed for the last time and already bereft of its shedplate is No 42079. The loco had a chequered history. Originally built at Brighton Works in January 1951, it was one of the batch transferred from the Southern to the London Midland Region in December 1959 in exchange for a similar number of Standard 2-6-4 tanks. Short spells at Chester, Willesden, Crewe North and Rugby preceded its move to the Manchester area.

10TH APRIL 1964 ● D. CASH

The 1.10pm Rochdale to Liverpool Exchange Fast often resulted in a Newton Heath tank arriving at the Merseyside terminus at the scheduled time of 2.42pm. Fairburn 2-6-4T No **42279** passes through Preston Road and is slowing as the train approaches Walton Junction on the last leg of its journey. The loco moved on to Neasden the following year. **20TH MARCH 1957** ● **J.A. PEDEN**

Parbold Station and Cabin looking east. Fairburn 2-6-4T No **42287** gets the 4.55pm Strike Special from Southport to Rochdale on its way. A breakdown of negotiations between the Associated Society of Locomotive Engineers and Firemen (ASLEF) and the British Transport Commission regarding differential wage structures resulted in strike action from midnight, 28th May until 6pm, 14th June 1955. Meanwhile, BR operated a rather erratic token service as the National Union of Railwaymen were not involved. **1ST JUNE 1955** ● **H.B. PRIESTLEY**

Another view of Fairburn 2-6-4T No 42696, this time employed as a pilot loco around the Oldham Loop as far as Rochdale. The train, starting out from Failsworth before picking up at other local stations, is a holiday special to Blackpool North and Fleetwood. The train loco is a Southport Class Five 4-6-0 No **45228** - no doubt borrowed by Newton Heath. The pair make a stirring sight leaving Royton Junction towards Shaw & Crompton, passing Royton Junction Sidings signalbox.

23RD JUNE 1962 ● D. CASH

A long iron footbridge that once offered pedestrians access to the town centre, linking Bolton Trinity Street with Johnson Street, was also an excellent vantage point to observe traffic movements at the north end of the station. On this occasion 2-6-4T No **2284**, still to be renumbered, is propelling the stock of a train from Manchester (or Rochdale) around the triangle *(above)* before drawing forward into the station for the return working *(right)*. This manoeuvre would save several moves, rather than run round and shunt to the other side of the station. A similar practice was also adopted at Todmorden with trains from the Burnley direction. The Bolton avoiding line - a 270 yard curve connecting the Blackburn and Preston lines, never carried a regular passenger service but was used by excursion trains from Blackburn and Darwen to Blackpool and Southport over the years.

28TH AUGUST 1948 ● B.K.B. GREEN

THE STANIER 2-6-4 TANKS

An Up stopping train from Blackburn to Manchester Victoria takes the direct route towards Pendleton (Old) Station at Agecroft Junction. Stanier tank No **42486** is in charge and passes alongside the *Manchester, Bolton and Bury Canal* at this point. The pair of cooling towers, a part of the Agecroft Power Station complex, epitomised the heavily industrialised area.   **15TH JUNE 1954** ● **B.K.B. GREEN**

The 1.19pm SO Rochdale to Liverpool Exchange Fast again with Stanier Tank power. 2-6-4T No **42614** takes the Wigan line at Lostock Junction. Having called at Bury Knowsley Street and Bolton, the only other stops were at Wigan (Wallgate) and Kirkby.
8TH FEBRUARY 1964 ● **E.F. BENTLEY**

A regular running-in turn for visiting locos to Derby Works was the 11.15am to Nottingham. 2-6-4T No **42621** leaves Derby Midland with the train, the leading two coaches being parcels vans. The bunker of a 'Jinty' 0-6-0 tank is prominent which appears to be on Station Pilot duty whilst a 4F 0-6-0 stands in the distance almost under the long footbridge offering official access to Derby Works and MPD.

19TH APRIL 1958 ● R.J. BUCKLEY

Passing Leyland with nine non-corridor coaches is 2-6-4T No **42623** on excursion work to Blackpool. By this time sorties to the coast by ex-L&Y 0-6-0's on trains such as this were virtually over. Newton Heath entrusted their tank engines or Ivatt 2-6-0's to supplement the larger 4-6-0's in times of shortage of suitable motive power. Bashall's Sidings signalbox and sidings, serving the nearby Leyland Motors complex is in view.

29TH MAY 1961 ● B.K.B. GREEN

Awaiting the signal at the east end of Platform 14 is Stanier 2-6-4T No **42660** The loco enjoyed two spells at Newton Heath - originally arriving in September 1956 from Chester. In January 1961 it moved across the city to Patricroft but returned in June 1964 for a further 7 month period.

1ST DECEMBER 1964 ● **G. COLTAS**

Replenishing the tanks at Rochdale Station after arrival with a Liverpool Exchange ▶ to Rochdale stopping train are the crew of Stanier 2-6-4T No **42622**. The fireman was responsible for climbing on to the tank top and positioning the water pipe (or bag as it was more commonly referred to) in the tank. The driver meanwhile controlled the water flow. This unusual view, which offers a wealth of detail for the modeller, was taken from the signal gantry at the north east end of Platforms 1 and 2. **c1958** ● **K. FIELD**

Hurrying into Castleton Station with the 11.40am SX Rochdale to Hellifield stopping train is No **42549**. This was usually a Lower Darwen or Hellifield loco, but as the day was Easter Monday, the inward working may have been cancelled (on Saturdays, the 11.40am went to Southport behind one of their locos). Beyond Castleton Station signalbox, one of four in the immediate vicinity, stands the textile machinery firm of Tweedale and Smalley whose chimney is prominent. Opposite their premises on the Up side of the line was Magee Marshall's malting house, both of which were rail-connected. This loco was an early casualty, being withdrawn in November 1961, having worked out of Accrington MPD during the BR period for almost a decade. Eighteen months later, the former L&Y signal box of 1896 vintage, which contained 20 levers, met a similar fate and was replaced by a ground frame.

18TH APRIL 1960 ● **R.S. GREENWOOD**

▼

Climbing the bank away from Hollinwood towards Oldham Werneth is 2-6-4T No **42624** with yet another Manchester Victoria to Rochdale local commuter train. The severe gradients on the Oldham Loop between Thorpes Bridge Junction and Royton Junction demanded that all Down excursions were double headed. Although a bleak location, this low angle view of the train nicely silhouettes the bogie wheels of the non-corridor stock with the inevitable cotton mill also prominent.　　　　　　　　　　　　　　　**JUNE 1958 ● D. CASH**

A Castleton to Belle Vue HALFEX in connection with a scout's jamboree, is pictured in more pleasant surroundings between New Hey and Shaw further around the Oldham Loop. 2-6-4T No **42620** is the loco. Amongst others, Nos 42618 - 42626 all featured on 26A's allocation at one time or another during the 1950/60's. This one was a late arrival though, having worked out of Accrington MPD prior to January 1960 although it stayed until withdrawal in September 1964.

25TH JUNE 1960 ● R.S. GREENWOOD

Departing from the east end of Oldham Mumps Station with a local stopping train and about to cross Whitehead Street bridge is 2-6-4T No **42660**. During 1957 the station facilities here benefitted from a major reconstruction, although they are far from evident in this view, taken from Oldham Mumps No 3 signalbox. Some 12 years later another significant development involved the rebuilding of the bridge and realignment of track which was in conjunction with road improvements. The signalbox had disappeared by this time as had the Rochdale bay, occupied by coaching stock on this occasion.

JUNE 1958 ● D. CASH

Caught between two moving trains on the permanent way resulted in this fine view of Hughes/Fowler 'Crab' 2-6-0 No **42707** on the Down Slow line near Euxton Junction. It was taken by local photographer Ray Farrell whose lineside permit allowed him to record such dramatic scenes - despite it being a summer Saturday on one of the busiest stretches of line in the north! The Reporting Number C259 indicated the train to be regularly scheduled and not an excursion (reporting numbers below 500 were only carried during holiday periods) and is a Summer Saturdays Only Fleetwood to Manchester train offering a connection from the Isle of Man.

25TH JULY 1959 ● R. FARRELL

THE HUGHES/FOWLER CRAB 2-6-0's

Shedmates meet deep in the heart of the Calder Valley near Hebden Bridge. 2-6-0 No **42750** works a Mytholmroyd to Moston freight which is the return working off the 6.15am Manchester Victoria to Bradford Exchange earlier in the day. The approaching WD 2-8-0 is No **90248,** heading north with a Brewery Sidings to Tees freight.

1960 ● J.A. COX

A most unlikely location to observe a Newton Heath 'Crab' would have to be Clowne, situated on the former Midland line between Staveley and Langwith Junction. The 2-6-0, No **42710** had even attracted the attention of a local lady, bag in hand and perhaps returning home after an afternoon's shopping. The train, showing Class A headlamps on the single line is the 10.50am Blackpool North - Radford.

1ST AUGUST 1959 ● **R.J. BUCKLEY**

A more familiar location was York's Racecourse Station with the imposing Holgate Bridge forming a backdrop - although usually associated with classic studies of Gresley Pacifics at work. The York Clifton Sidings to Red Bank empty newspaper vans was often entrusted to a single locomotive as far as Leeds on Saturdays and here, No **42715** works the train during its formative period of operation.

27TH AUGUST 1955 ● **J. PEDEN**

Having brought a Sunday Excursion train to the Derbyshire Spa town of Buxton, 2-6-0 No **42878** is on the Buxton Curve in the process of stabling the empty stock. The leading carriage - the only one in view - is of CLC origin. The train has originated from the Central Division, probably the Oldham district, and will have arrived over ex-LNWR metals by way of Denton Junction, Stockport Edgeley Junction and the direct branch.

19TH AUGUST 1951 ● **E.R. MORTEN**

The freshly ballasted track between Broadley and Whitworth is in the process of being treated to a liberal sprinkling of weedkiller. The spray in fact extended beyond this to help arrest the spread of vegetation along the little used branch line from Rochdale to Facit. Brake vans are at either end but within the train are a pair of suitably converted carriages of Gresley vintage which appear to be carrying roofboards! Long standing Newton Heath 2-6-0 No **42750** makes deliberately slow progress whilst sporting an unfamiliar Reporting Number - 6Z07.

30TH APRIL 1963 ● **R.S. GREENWOOD**

A wonderfully composed railway photograph illustrating elements of railway infrastructure so often ignored by the cameraman in favour of the locomotive and train. 'Crab' 2-6-0 No **42714** approaching Turton and Edgworth Station (closed 5th February 1961) with the 5.40pm (SX) Manchester Victoria to Hellifield is merely part of the evocative scene, so typical of many secondary lines, now lost for ever. Other intermediate stations north of Blackburn closed at the end of the 1962 summer timetable with the consequent loss of workings. Newton Heath engines and men had regular work as far as Hellifield but No 42714, now surplus to requirements, was withdrawn in October 1962. Many years earlier it had the distinction of working the last stopping train to run eastbound over the Spen Valley line - the 9.15pm (SO) Manchester Victoria to Leeds City on 3rd October 1953. **8TH AUGUST 1962** ● **E.F. BENTLEY**

Approaching Bradley Fold Station are Engine and Brake Van heading eastbound. The 2-6-0 is No **42710** whilst the brake van, of LMS origin, is now restricted to ballast and permanent way trains. Work is taking place on the signalbox, its lower half being strengthened with the original timbers being replaced by brick. The Civil Engineers Department were responsible for this before handing over to the Signal and Telegraph Department who will install a new lead off frame outside the box. Concrete trestles and lengths of 12" x 6" creosoted timber have been delivered for the purpose. The Bolton S & T signal gang's mess coach is already in attendance. **25TH FEBRUARY 1963** ● **E.F. BENTLEY**

The Blackpool holiday traffic accounted for the movements of many of 26A's 'Crabs'. No **42707** passes through Farington with a Blackpool - Cleethorpes train. The route is via the ex-L&Y line through Manchester Victoria, up Miles Platting bank (with rear assistance), Philips Park and Midland Junction where steam gave way to electric traction. Onward progress is via Sheffield Victoria and Lincoln Central. **1ST AUGUST 1959** ● **B.W.L. BROOKSBANK**

Another summer Saturday extra working brings 2-6-0 No **42715** on to the North Wales coast. The train, which is nearing Llandudno Junction station, is showing Western Lines Reporting Number W459, which indicates it being the 11.25am Manchester Exchange to Llandudno. Another train of mixed stock heads away towards Chester whilst trailing in on the right is a branch line service from Blaenau Ffestiniog hauled by an Ivatt 2-6-2T. **4TH AUGUST 1951** ● **B.W.L. BROOKSBANK**

Rattling over the arm of the Rochdale Canal tender first with a fully laden mineral train is 'Crab' 2-6-0 No **42714**. This is the east end of Rochdale Station where Ivatt 2-6-0 No **46406** is also in attendance on Pilot duties. Immediately left of the tender is a rail connected warehouse where the hoists and capstans in the goods yard were driven from a water accumulator visible in the background. The station lifts were similarly operated. Directly over the leading wagon stands the small Goods Yard Signalbox.

2ND OCTOBER 1959 ● **R.S. GREENWOOD**

Toiling north through a deserted Wilpshire Station with a mixed freight is 2-6-0 No **42733**.   **18TH JUNE 1962** ● **R.S. GREENWOOD**

Passing Under Crescent Bridge, Peterborough, and well off the beaten track is 2-6-0 No **42708.** The engine, showing a single lamp, seems to indicate a mixed train in this case as a van appears behind the tender although the working remains a mystery. The exact location is just south of Peterborough North Station on the ex-LNER main line. The loco ventured even further afield in early 1953 when it went north of the border to Thornton Junction MPD (62A) with shed-mates Nos 42871/8. This was to assist with the annual seed potato traffic, but in addition, the depot utilised them on other work. For example No 42708 was observed on several occasions heading the 5.10pm Edinburgh Waverley to Dundee via Crail - normally an ex-LNER B1 turn. All three returned home after a few weeks, but the moves were classed as official transfers as distinct from loans.

c1957 ● AUTHOR'S COLLECTION

An early morning sun nicely highlights the wheels and motion of 2-6-0 No **42726.** The train is the 8.20am Bolton Trinity Street to Manchester Victoria calling all stations and arriving at 8.43am - the location is Rose Hill.

19TH APRIL 1960 ● D. HAMPSON

On more familiar territory, plying their trade up and down the Calder Valley with a constant procession of mineral trains. Returning eastbound empties from the Manchester area for the Yorkshire coalfield is 2-6-0 No **42715.** The four track section is near Hebden Bridge.

10TH JULY 1959 ● B.W.L. BROOKSBANK

A view of the return working off the 6.15am Manchester Victoria - Bradford Exchange. On this occasion 2-6-0 No **42710** brings the coal train from Mytholmroyd past the former down platform at Smithy Bridge. When the station reopened in 1985, the down platform was built on the other side of the level crossing. **24TH MARCH 1962** ● **R.S. GREENWOOD**

A returning holiday extra from Bournemouth to Castleton has been re-routed clockwise around the Oldham Loop due to the unavailability of a pilot engine. 'Crab' 2-6-0 No **42750** passes Milnrow between Rochdale and Oldham with a typical scratch set of carriages, the rearmost of which are crossing the River Beal. **18TH AUGUST 1962** ● **R.S. GREENWOOD**

The conveyance of perishables represented a considerable source of revenue for the rail companies over many years until the early 1960s when refrigerated road transport became a more viable alternative. The L&Y were fortunate in being able to transport fish in large quantities from both east and west coasts and in 1912 developed a large market at Wyre Dock, Fleetwood. This was capable of accommodating many vessels which resulted in hundreds of basses of freshly caught fish being forwarded overnight all over the country. One of the surviving workings was the Saturdays Only Fleetwood to Oldham train which ran via Bury (Knowsley Street) thus avoiding the congested Manchester area. Approaching Euxton Junction with the short train is 'Crab' 2-6-0 No **42733**, casting a pronounced shadow on the embankment. Present are a group of trainspotters, doubtless kept occupied observing the frequent procession of trains hauled by an interesting selection of engines. The strong afternoon sun would result in a few ruddy faces at the end of the day! **13TH JULY 1963** ● **I.G. HOLT**

The previous Saturday, the same locomotive had been employed on the Scotswood - Red Bank empty vans which it worked single handed between York and Leeds City where a pilot engine was usually attached. 2-6-0 No **42733** works south away from the Minster City and has reached Copmanthorpe, a notorious race track where in days of old, the LMS and LNER went head to head after simultaneous departures from York station. Such rivalries extended well into the BR period. **6TH JULY 1963** ● **I.G. HOLT**

The winter of the 1960's deep freeze. Conditions were particularly bleak between Christmas 1962 and the New Year of 1963, but those intrepid souls who were willing to brave the elements were often rewarded with dramatic results. An empty coal train from Middleton Junction to Healey Mills makes steady progress shortly after passing Rochdale East Junction. The loco is 2-6-0 No **42704**.

28TH DECEMBER 1962 ● **R.S. GREENWOOD**

Approaching Jubilee Accommodation Crossing between New Hey and Shaw is a Blackpool Central to Oldham return holiday train with 'Crab' 2-6-0 No **42705**. The stock is a typical non-corridor set, stabled at Lightbowne for the greater part of the year.

25TH JUNE 1960 ● **R.S. GREENWOOD**

Easter Monday morning excursion traffic in the Calder Valley. A Chesterfield to Blackpool North train passes through Walsden behind Sheffield Darnall B1 4-6-0 No **61109**. The ex-LNER loco meets a Newton Heath 2-6-0 No **42714** heading east with empty stock from Lightbowne Sidings to Todmorden from where it will form an excursion to Southport. The first coach appears to be part of a Gresley articulated non-corridor 'twin'.

23RD APRIL 1962 ● **R.S. GREENWOOD**

At the time of the formation of British Railways in 1948, a total of 19 members of the Hughes/Fowler 2-6-0 class were on Newton Heath's allocation - a number only exceeded by nearby Agecroft MPD (21). They were versatile locos and generally popular with crews and their mixed traffic status made them eminently suitable for the diversity of work at 26A. Approaching Middleton Junction Station and passing under clear signals with an eastbound mixed freight, the loco still carries its LMS number - **2702** which many did in those early post nationalisation days. The left and right arms of the splitting signal designated the lines to Oldham via the Werneth Incline and the Middleton Branch respectively.

c.1950 ● J. DAVENPORT

THE STANIER 2-6-0's

Adding further variety to the locomotive scene at Newton Heath during the BR period were two Stanier 2-6-0's, commonly referred to as Stanier 'Crabs'. They arrived to supplement the allocation for the summer months of 1959, a task often performed by the Jubilees (see page 78). Nos 42963 and 42970 arrived during June from Crewe (North) and Birkenhead MPD's respectively. The beginning of the winter timetable heralded their return in September. No **42963** is in charge of the 6.00pm Rochdale - Hellifield freight at Castleton.

26TH AUGUST 1959 ●
R.S. GREENWOOD

Three days later and the same loco is working the 5.35pm Manchester Victoria to Todmorden stopping train, which was a regular Newton Heath duty on Saturdays only. No **42963** makes steady progress between Castleton and Rochdale. The Stanier 'Crabs' were something of a rarity on the Central Division as the class of forty locos tended to operate over the former LNWR lines in later years. Built at Crewe in 1933/4, their original power classification was 4F, becoming 5P4F shortly after introduction - then 5P5F and finally 5F before Nationalisation. There was a discrepancy in width of engine and tender which was similar to that of Jubilees when paired with Fowler's 3,500 examples. This particular loco had the distinction of being the last of its class to be withdrawn in 1966 whilst another member, No 42968 survives in preservation.

29TH AUGUST 1959 ● R.S. GREENWOOD

THE FOWLER 4F 0-6-0's

Veteran ex-Midland 0-6-0 No 44022, working tender first, ambles along the main line approaching Castleton Sidings with a short mixed goods train consisting of nine wagons and brake van. This photograph nicely illustrates the variety of merchandise conveyed from Brewery Sidings to Rochdale by rail as no two wagons appear to be similar.   **27TH AUGUST 1960** ● **R.S. GREENWOOD**

During the 1950s, Newton Heath had three Fowler 4F 0-6-0's to augment its stud of ex L&YR 3F 0-6-0's for local trip and shunting work. No 44022 was a relative newcomer arriving in March 1956 upon the closure of the nearby ex MR Belle Vue shed. Nos **44311** and 44543 had been there since LMS days, together with Nos 44056 and 44544 and one wonders how the older 'Lanky' men took to them. Both locos had tender cabs with frames suitably modified for snow plough usage. 44311's history was notable. The loco moved on in June 1961 via Bury and Bolton before arriving at Barrow in November 1965. Together with No 44500, they were the last two examples of a class originally numbering 772 to be withdrawn from capital stock on 9th July 1966. On a summer Saturday in 1960, the shed was typically hard pressed to find sufficient motive power to satisfy the extra excursion traffic. No 44311 was put into service and is seen here leaving Kirkham, safety valves blowing, on the Down slow line with a train signalled to Blackpool North. One also wonders whether the prefix 'C' of the reporting number C703 made it to the coast!   **2ND JULY 1960** ● **P. FITTON**

It was necessary for signalmen operating the boxes at Rochdale West Junction, East Junction and Goods Yard to be able to offer a clear road through the station environs for the stiff gradient to Milnrow Road bridge for this particular working. No **44311** has charge of a train of 'cripples' from Brewery Sidings to Royton Junction which consisted of a motley collection of wagons destined to be classified for repair or scrap. Foggy weather and a greasy rail hardly helped matters.

27TH NOVEMBER 1959 ●
R.S. GREENWOOD

A fine summer Saturday morning at Castleton sees 0-6-0 No **44431** drifting by, working tender first with empty carriage stock from Lightbowne Sidings, directly opposite the loco's home shed. This will form a Rochdale to Southport excursion later in the day.

20TH AUGUST 1960 ●
R.S. GREENWOOD

Departure time approaches for the 5.15pm SO Rochdale - Wigan Wallgate three coach local train. The loco entrusted to the duty is No **44543**, which moved to Newton Heath from neighbouring Agecroft week ending March 12th 1949. Film buffs might recall *The Love Match* starring Arthur Askey who, cast as an engine driver, featured in several scenes with this engine. Memorable clips show him on location at 26A and a closing sequence overlooking the packed terraces of Burnden Park, close to Burnden Junction on the Bury line which was the home of Bolton Wanderers football club during the days of steam.

10TH OCTOBER 1959 ● **R.S. GREENWOOD**

Cotton mills **Lily and Briar** dominate the scene looking back towards Shaw and Crompton Station from Linney Lane bridge. No **44543** gets underway past the goods yard with a Manchester Victoria to Rochdale commuter train via Oldham. A portion of the imposing goods warehouse is visible and also of interest is a long train of flat wagons containing new tractor units held in the Down loop.

4TH JULY 1958 ● P. HUTCHINSON

The 11.47am SO Bolton Trinity Street to Leeds Central train was one of only three through workings into Yorkshire off the Bolton line. No **44022**, passes Gypsy Lane, shortly after calling at Castleton bound for Rochdale. The other services were a Summer Saturdays Only Liverpool Exchange to Scarborough and return and a Sunday night only Liverpool Exchange to York which ran non stop between Bolton and Rochdale conveying service personnel en route back to camp in Yorkshire after weekend leave.

16TH JULY 1960 ● R.S. GREENWOOD

Up until early **1960,** this ex-Midland Railway loco remained coupled to a tender of similar origin. No **44022** gravitated to Newton Heath with the closure of Belle Vue MPD on 15th April 1956 and, perhaps surprisingly, became highly regarded by some of the locomen there. It was regularly rostered and remained a well travelled engine right up until withdrawal in November 1963 having been observed on Leeds (Holbeck) and Royston MPD's shortly beforehand. Six weeks later it succumbed to the cutter's torch at Horwich. The 0-6-0 is working the evening Broadfield - Rochdale freight with traffic mainly from RAF 35 Maintenance Unit Heywood, and is approaching Castleton Sidings, New Barn Lane, Rochdale.

26TH AUGUST 1959 ● R.S. GREENWOOD

Engaged in a spot of Station Pilot work at Manchester Victoria East Junction is former Midland 0-6-0 No **43952.** This veteran arrived from Wigan (L&Y) in the company of No 44221 during December 1962, but apparently did little work during its stay. The loco stayed on the Central Division, transferring to Lower Darwen a year later.　　**17TH MARCH 1963** ● **G. COLTAS**

The River Wye flows deep below Monsal Head viaduct through the pretty Monsal Dale, situated between Bakewell and Millers Dale. No **44543** rolls off at the north end with a freight bound for the Manchester area. The men who worked the Rowsley Link were mainly involved with overnight fully fitted freights from Moston Sidings, Philips Park or Ancoats by way of the ex-Midland main line as far as Rowsley Exchange Sidings. A few may have even appreciated the scenery during their return journey in daylight.

c.1958 ● **A.G. ELLIS**

A Good Friday excursion from Failsworth to Blackpool leaves Milnrow station behind No **44431** and train engine, shedmate No **45101**. The 4F 0-6-0 paid a second visit to the Oldham line later that day - acting as pilot once more to a returning rugby league special from Swinton to Oldham.

20TH APRIL 1962 ● **R.S. GREENWOOD**

The ex-Belle Vue engine, No 44022 was a regular performer over the Oldham Loop, assisting with all manner of excursion traffic. On this occasion it is piloting a commendably clean Class Five 4-6-0 No **45290** (26A) with an Oldham Werneth to Millom excursion on the approach to New Hey. The next frame *(below)* reveals Two Bridges Road bridge in the distance, beyond which are the station and its environs. The spire of the imposing St. Thomas' Church is visible above the 4F's exhaust but the other landmark, the large ex-L&Y goods warehouse, situated on the Down side opposite the platforms, is not.   **17TH APRIL 1960** ● **R.S. GREENWOOD**

Having just passed the throat of Lees (Oldham) shed, No 44543 is about to either pass under Oldham Road bridge in the Greenfield direction or reverse over the crossover in the foreground on to the Down line before passing through Lees station in the direction of Oldham.

c1956 ● J. DAVENPORT

The line from Oldham Clegg Street by way of Park Bridge and OA&GB junction was a convenient route for Manchester bound parcels traffic. No 44311 continues its journey through the semi rural district of Droylsden with an interesting assortment of vans. The train will shortly cross the Medlock Viaduct before passing through Clayton Bridge Station and Philips Park.

c1954 ● J. DAVENPORT

Assisting with the extra volume of parcels traffic brought about by a rapidly approaching Christmas is 4F No 44221. This is Manchester Victoria's Platform 11 Middle which, as well as providing a link with the adjacent Exchange Station, dealt with all manner of parcels and newspaper traffic. The glass screen beyond the canopy offered a degree of protection from the elements to both staff and the seemingly endless sacks of parcels. Few passenger trains actually used this middle section other than the regular morning (9.30am) and afternoon (4.10pm) Glasgow trains which then departed through the centre road at Exchange Station.

16TH DECEMBER 1962 ●
AUTHOR'S COLLECTION

The intensive passenger services between Manchester, the Fylde coast and Southport resulted in a large number of Class Fives regularly entrusted to these duties - but not exclusively so. No **44890**, which spent the entire BR period at Newton Heath up to its withdrawal in June 1968, departs under clear signals from Lostock Junction with the 1.40pm Manchester Victoria - Blackpool North and Fleetwood slow. The Wigan line diverges to the right beyond the inclined pathway leading to the station entrance. **8TH FEBRUARY 1964** ● **E.F. BENTLEY**

THE STANIER CLASS FIVE 4-6-0's

Despite large numbers of the class being allocated to Newton Heath, very few actually passed the depot on regular passenger workings. On this occasion No **45225** is unusually employed on a Liverpool Exchange - Bradford Exchange /Leeds Central express and has probably been borrowed by Bank Hall MPD. The train is passing through Newton Heath station and is about to cross the 'hoop bridge' over St Mary's Road. It will then pass through Moston and Middleton Junction before reaching Rochdale, its first stop out of Manchester Victoria.

c1956 ● **J. DAVENPORT**

The 4.58pm all stations from Wellingborough to Leicester was renowned for producing a variety of locos. The working attracted amongst others - Class 2P 4-4-0's, Compounds, 4F 0-6-0's, the occasional Jubilee and Class Fives. The loco came off Wellingborough shed after lunch to pick up the empty stock at the carriage sidings where it would idle the afternoon away. A most unprecedented visitor was No **45156 *Ayrshire Yeomanry,*** recently transferred from St Rollox (Glasgow) to Newton Heath, seen departing amidst a scene that is pure Midland Railway nostalgia.   **31ST MAY 1957 ● K. FAIREY**

The same loco similarly deployed three months ▷ later on a stopping train during the evening rush hour. The 4.55pm Middleton Junction to Rochdale was now home territory for No **45156 *Ayrshire Yeomanry*** which had travelled via the notorious Werneth Incline to Oldham then around the loop to Rochdale. Still in presentable condition, the engine is caught leaving Shaw and Crompton Station.

28TH AUGUST 1957 ● H.B. PRIESTLEY

A visit to Crewe Works, as distinct from St Rollox, resulted in the loss of its large cabside numerals. The 'ferret and dartboard' totem was replaced in favour of the newer pattern but No **45156** managed to retain its original front numberplate with serif characters. ***Ayrshire Yeomanry,*** now looking decidedly worse for wear, is once more engaged on a stopping train - the 11.00am Rochdale to Liverpool Exchange, seen passing Winstanley Colliery Sidings, Wigan.

4TH NOVEMBER 1961 ● A.C. GILBERT
▽

The 3.10pm Manchester Victoria to Blackpool stopping train split at Kirkham with the front portion for Central and rear for North stations. A rather grimy member, No **44696** continues via the coast line with the first three carriages and passes Moss Side signalbox and over the level crossing carrying the B5259 road. The station, situated between Wrea Green and Lytham had closed two years previously on 26th June 1961. **14TH SEPTEMBER 1963 ● P. FITTON**

A returning Scarborough to Manchester Victoria excursion is near Marsden, high on the hills with No **45435** on the approach to the 3 mile long Standedge Tunnel. The original LNWR Leeds to Manchester route of 1849 was double track apart from the tunnel itself which was single. A second bore opened in 1871 to relieve congestion but the continued increase in traffic resulted in the lines quadrupling between Huddersfield and Stalybridge with a third tunnel of double track bore opening in 1895. The lines to the right of the train, largely used by freight, ran through the original tunnels to Diggle and south to Stalybridge by way of the newer Micklehurst Loop. This ran close by the original route but the terrain precluded the widening of this section.

10TH OCTOBER 1953 ● B.K.B. GREEN

An unusual Saturday morning visitor to Skipton was Class Five No **45246**. The 9D engine had arrived at 11.35am with a mere four carriages which comprised a Manchester Victoria to Gourock special (1P51). Engine and stock stand amidst the rather attractive canopies at Skipton Station, awaiting the arrival of Jubilee No 45608 *Gibraltar* with the Leeds portion for Gourock in the opposite direction. The combined train departed at 12.02pm (Reporting Number 1S43) behind the Holbeck loco to do battle over the Settle and Carlisle route to Carlisle.

19TH JUNE 1965 ● P. FITTON

Signalled for the Stoke line, Class Five No **44736** approaches Cheadle Hulme with the 12.10pm Manchester London Road to Birmingham. The rear-most coaches have just cleared Ladybridge Viaduct, known locally as *Seven Arches,* which spans the Ladybrook valley. The loco is in ex-works condition and is undoubtedly on a running-in turn.

27TH FEBRUARY 1955 ● B.K.B. GREEN

The diminutive Scout Green signal box became redundant on 15th April 1973 with the opening of the new power facility at Preston. Having stood since 1871 it would have witnessed the passing of many a Newton Heath loco slogging north up the formidable Shap incline. A Manchester Victoria to Keswick train made up of six coaches presented no such problems for the crew of Class Five No **44697** and reached the summit in fine style, passing at 12.52pm. It is one of four fitted with a self weighing tender, all of which were based on the LMR.

15TH AUGUST 1964 ● P. FITTON
▼

A northbound excursion awaits departure from Wigan (North Western) Station on a fine summer's evening at 7.50pm. The pilot loco is Rose Grove's No **45216** and the train engine, 26A's No **44845** which is in the process of having its tender replenished and possibly causing the delay. Newton Heath locos were an every day sight in the town, mainly over ex-L&Y lines on Southport and Liverpool trains which were served by the nearby Wallgate Station. They were less frequently observed on this portion of the ex-LNWR main line.

3RD JUNE 1965 ● E.F. BENTLEY
▼

The shed had a two-year flirtation with the Caprotti variety in the form of No **44746.** The loco arrived during April 1960 after spending a similar period at Longsight but previous to this had worked largely on the Midland main line out of Bristol (Barrow Road) and Leeds (Holbeck). Reporting Number W514 was a returning Morecambe - Oldham holiday relief seen here at Goats Bridge, Shaw with both driver and fireman mindful of the cameraman's presence.   **25TH JUNE 1960** ● **R.S.GREENWOOD**

A pair of Stanier Class Fives conspire to pollute the Farnley district of Leeds. The train is a Hull to Liverpool Lime Street express and is traversing the new line from Leeds City Station to Farnley Junction. No **45105** (26A) is piloting No **45305** (5B - since preserved) and may be making its way back to Newton Heath from an unbalanced working. Two of the distinctive liveried vans belonging to local biscuit manufacturer *Meredith and Drew* can be glimpsed in the yard in the right foreground. The pungent, sulphurous smells from the engines would have offered a stark, but no less enjoyable contrast to that of freshly baked biscuits!   **10TH JUNE 1957** ● **B.K.B. GREEN**

An Easter Monday day trip to Blackpool remained a family tradition for generations of Lancashire and Yorkshire public alike. Passengers on this train would be none too pleased though. The 1X07 Doncaster to Blackpool North was running late and it was already 1.35pm when Class Five No **44891** piloting Stanier 2-6-0 No **42945** passed Singleton Box, near Poulton. The excursion had travelled over Woodhead, hauled by electric traction before handing over to the Mogul at Midland Junction, Manchester near which, was its home shed - Gorton. The loco failed at Adlington and No 44891 was commandeered to assist to the coast. In all probability, this was the Stanier 'Crab's' last attempt at passenger work. Gorton shed closed two months later and the forerunner of the class ended its days at Heaton Mersey.

19TH APRIL 1965 ● P. FITTON

The driver looking back down his train and awaiting the off is undoubtedly a Willesden man as Class Five No **44893** is standing at Harrow & Wealdstone Station with a stopping train to Bletchley. This was a typical filling-in turn out of the London depot which regularly utilised the visiting locomotive off the Moston - Camden overnight fitted freight.

1956 ● AUTHOR'S COLLECTION

The line between Greenfield Junction and OAGB Junction via Oldham Glodwick Road, Clegg Street and Park Bridge was a convenient diversionary route when engineering work was in progress in the Stalybridge and Mossley area. The gradients on the line often demanded a pilot loco and Newton Heath usually provided the motive power. 4-6-0 No **44933** assists Edge Hill Jubilee 4-6-0 No **45567** *South Australia* with a Newcastle - Liverpool Lime Street express near Park Bridge.

10TH JULY 1955 ● J. DAVENPORT

Bolton East Junction. The early evening sun nicely catches Stanier Class Five No **45233** as the driver shuts off steam on the approaches to Trinity Street Station. The train is the 6.30pm Manchester Victoria to Blackburn semi fast, stopping only at Bolton and Darwen. Disappearing in the opposite direction is the 4.55pm Fleetwood, 5.10pm Blackpool North to Manchester Victoria hauled by another Class Five. Meanwhile a Hughes/Fowler 'Crab' 2-6-0 lurks in Haslam's Sidings awaiting a path to work a short transfer freight to Halliwell Goods. Lever Street footbridge, from where the photograph was taken, afforded excellent views of the junction in either direction.

17TH MAY 1963 ● **E.F. BENTLEY**

Immediately east of Rochdale the main line runs level for 2 miles before the long ascent into Yorkshire begins. Clegg Hall Troughs, situated on this section, is the location for named Class Five No **45154 Lanarkshire Yeomanry.** The train is an Inter-Regional excursion.

20TH MAY 1961 ● **R.S. GREENWOOD**

Class Five No 45246 takes the Bury line at Burnden Junction, Bolton with a mixed goods destined for Royton Junction. In 1962 the former North British Railway workshops at Cowlairs, Glasgow, became part of BR Workshops Division and as a consequence a number of engines based in England went north of the border for repair. They often emerged with the Cowlairs 'trademark', derived from LNER practice - the home shed applied in white on a repainted red buffer beam - such was the case with No 45246 after shopping. The engine was previously allocated to Carlisle Upperby MPD throughout the 1950's until its transfer to Newton Heath in June 1963.

28TH DECEMBER 1963 ● D.A. HAMPSON

Sauntering through Littleborough with a mineral train from the Yorkshire coalfield is No **45232**. By 1961 Newton Heath had a veritable army of Class Fives and they could always be found on these more humble duties.

20TH MAY 1961 ● I.G. HOLT

An unusual choice of motive power for the 10.35am Carnforth to Leeds City is No **45104**. The train is on time, passing Hellifield one hour after departure.

4TH JUNE 1963 ● P. FITTON

The Euxton Junction signalman rolls up his green flag having waved the 2.15pm Manchester Victoria - Glasgow Central forward around the curve from the Chorley direction to join the main line. The crew of No **44891,** having reached a standstill, would have been made aware of the situation beforehand but a verbal instruction as to which road they would take would be conveyed from the signalman. The splitting signal for the Down Fast and Slow lines between here and Preston had recently lost its distant arms and was possibly out of order.

9TH JULY 1966 ● R. FARRELL

A popular vantage point was Oldham Road Bridge which provided an elevated view of the Oldham, Ashton and Guide Bridge Junction (OA&GB Jct). No **45031,** a Class Five that flew the nest to Mold Junction in January 1960, heads towards Leeds and will shortly pass through Ashton Charlestown Station. The lines trailing in from the left beyond the bridge are from Crowthorne Junction, which in turn offered a choice of route to Denton and Stockport, or Guide Bridge. Those in the right foreground are for Oldham Clegg Street, via Ashton Oldham Road and Park bridge - a route which was generally known as the 'Park Bridge line'. The tall ex-L&Y signalbox, built to overlook both junctions was eventually replaced with a BR standard version on the opposite side of the line. **JULY 1958 ● J. DAVENPORT**

Newton Heath's engines and men had regular workings and lodging turns to London. The daily fitted freights from Moston Exchange Sidings to Camden and return Camden to Brewery Sidings alternated between Willesden and 26A locos. Both depots largely used Class Fives but Crabs and the occasional Jubilee amongst others also appeared. No **45104** has found its way on to the Southern Region after having been borrowed by Willesden to work a cross-London freight. It has arrived at Norwood Junction, having arrived off the LMR via Crystal Palace.

8TH OCTOBER 1952 ● T.C. COLE

Another Class Five deep in Southern Region territory. In May 1953 seven of the class from various LMR depots were loaned to the region whilst their own Merchant Navy Pacifics were temporarily withdrawn from service as major problems had arisen with the driving axles. No **45223** found itself temporarily allocated to Bournemouth whilst retaining its 26A shedplate. It regularly worked the tightly timed expresses to and from London Waterloo and the South West and is seen here departing from Bournemouth Central with the 9.30am from London Waterloo to Bournemouth West express displaying the appropriate SR headcode discs.

23RD MAY 1953 ● F.W. DIXON

The Summer Saturdays Only Scarborough to Liverpool Exchange train bursts under Ainsworth Road bridge and through Radcliffe Black Lane Station on its way towards Bolton. 4-6-0 No **44735** is the locomotive assigned to the task. The platforms were staggered here, the station buildings being on the Bury side of the bridge. The compact waiting room on the Down platform is just visible through the arch as is the Black Lane cotton mill whose buildings stood adjacent to the railway. **21ST JULY 1962 ● I.G. HOLT**

The Manchester Wednesday League X1 was a football team drawn strictly from the employees at the depot and lasted from early L&Y days until the BR period. Their biggest day out in recent times came at the end of the 1951-52 season when they reached the final of the LMR Cup. Their opponents were Wolverton Town, a team formed by the staff at the carriage works with the match being played at Crewe Alexandra's Gresty Road ground. Support was such that the depot were able to provide transport for both team and supporters in the form of headboarded Class Five No **44696** and nine carriages. The train departed from Newton Heath Station (probably the only one ever to do so) and ran via India Rubber Junction (Miles Platting), Droylsden and Denton Junction thence via Stockport. Whether the loco was serviced on Crewe North or South shed remains unrecorded (the ground was midway between both), but the result was a convincing 4 - 2 win. Perhaps Jubilee No 45712 *Victory*, which was on the books at the time, might have been a more appropriate locomotive for the return trip! The history of the *Newton Heath Cricket and Football Club*, formed by a group of locomen in 1879 and the subsequent formation of *Manchester United Football Club* in 1902 have both been documented.

5TH MAY 1952 ● A. BENDELL

Awaiting the arrival of a southbound train from Scotland, immaculate Class Five No **44734** stands by ready to relieve in the centre road at Carlisle Citadel Station. It was the home depot's responsibility to provide the Reporting Number board affixed to the smokebox door and these were not to be transferred from engine to engine. 'C774' would be clearly stamped 'property of 26A' on the rear. The Class 2P 4-4-0 in the rear would probably be the standby engine from Upperby and on many occasions it was called on to assist an ailing Jubilee or Clan on the Manchester and Liverpool trains.

30TH AUGUST 1958 ● AUTHOR'S COLLECTION

Drifting past Handforth Sidings Signal Box ▶ with freight destined for Basford Hall Sidings is No **45233.** On the approach to Crewe, it would run by way of the Up independent line, thus bypassing the station and commonly referred to as 'the muck hole'.

22ND APRIL 1951 ● T. LEWIS

With the Hilton House Distant signal in its favour, No **44895** brings the 9.47am Manchester Victoria to Blackpool Central (SX) past the site of Dicconson Lane and Aspull (closed 1st February 1954). Calling at Walkden, Atherton and Preston only, this train was one of several using the line to Horwich Fork Junction thus bypassing the busy environs of Bolton. The other signal in view is the splitting distant for Hindley and Blackrod Branch Junction.   **26TH AUGUST 1964 ● B.G. BARLOW**

Waiting in the sidings, or the 'slums' as they were locally referred to, at Stockport Edgeley Station are a few parcels vans, the nearest of which appears to be of North Eastern origin. No **45076** is at their head. The station is in the process of renovation and the transverse ridge and furrow canopies protecting the platforms are in the process of demolition. Although the overhead catenary had been recently erected with the wires ready in place, the inaugural 25kV AC electric train service between Manchester Piccadilly and Crewe was still 4 months away. Whilst the power remained off, the locomotive was not yet strictly 'under the wires' and the electrification warning signs remain conspicuous by their absence.

28TH MAY 1960 ● G. WHITEHEAD

The Thames - Clyde Express which ran between London St. Pancras and Glasgow St. Enoch was usually in the hands of Holbeck's Jubilees south of Leeds. Extra loading on certain summer Saturdays resulted in relief trains running in both directions. How Newton Heath's engines ended up on such duties often remains shrouded in mystery. The likely explanation is that No **45233** had been borrowed by Holbeck to work forward from Leeds City - if indeed, the train had travelled throughout from Glasgow. One might also wonder as to whether the Class Five reached St. Pancras. The scratch set of coaches were a poor second to the main formation including restaurant car which preceded it. The Up relief is approaching Dore and Totley, some four miles south of Sheffield (Midland) with Beauchief Station barely visible beyond the distant bridge.

27TH JUNE 1953 ● B. GOODLAD

A heavy overnight frost nicely highlights the Permanent Way within the proximity of Bury Knowsley Street Station. This area was renowned by enginemen for its 'Bury hollow' - an abrupt change of gradient which may be detected between the third and fourth carriages of the incoming train. Class Five No **45101** arrives with the 9.15am Liverpool Exchange to Rochdale express which was a regular 26A duty. The trio of bridges in view are of interest. That in the distance carries the electrified line serving Bury Bolton Street Station upon which a Metro Cammell DMU passes by. The double arches over which Manchester Road crosses are next. A spur connecting both stations passes through the second arch whilst that nearest is Knowsley Street Bridge. High above, a capping stone is clearly dated 1848, coinciding with the opening of the station, whilst the footbridge is of relatively recent construction.   **17TH FEBRUARY 1962 ● R.S. GREENWOOD**

Dispelling the myth that the sun never shone in Manchester is this scene at Victoria Station. By this time there remained little variety amongst locomotive classes and Newton Heath still had sufficient Class Fives to cover many of their remaining steam turns. No **45101** whose cab is shrouded in steam, acts as Wallside Pilot whilst No **44803** is also on pilot duty, dealing with vans in Platform 11. The Blackpool trains were now composed of DMUs as witnessed between the engines departing from Platform 12.   **29TH JULY 1967 ● T. HEAVYSIDE**

Engine and brake saunter across the Tonge Viaduct
on the approaches to Bradshawgate Tunnel and Bolton from
the direction of Bromley Cross. The Class Five is No **44893**
and the lone pedestrian walking down Union Road appears
oblivious to its passing.

31ST AUGUST 1964 ● D.A. HAMPSON

An early photograph of the BR period records a Class ▶
Five still carrying its LMS number **5232**, shunting in the
Stalybridge area on the former LNWR route to Leeds.

JUNE 1948 ● G. WHITEHEAD

The evening Nelson to Moston van train was a regular duty for 26A locos and men. Trusty Class Five No **44803** passes through the
Up platform at Ramsbottom with the working on time at 6.15pm. The weed-infested scene suggests that both the former ELR warehouse
and the station sidings are now out of use, although the few vans that languish confirm the track remains in situ. Access from the goods yard
to the adjoining Down platform is by way of a bridge of sleepers whilst the prominent sign reads 'No engine allowed to enter the warehouse',
a highly desirable piece of railway memorabilia in today's market.　　　**22ND AUGUST 1963 ● E.F. BENTLEY**

The rear coach of the 5.55pm Blackpool Central to Wigan via the Marton line has just cleared Bloomfield Road bridge as the train makes haste towards Blackpool South. The impressive exhaust no doubt pleased the photographer but would be frowned upon by control whose local ruling was to keep smoke emissions in the area to a minimum. Class Five No **44697** is attached to a self weighing tender used in fuel consumption trials for many years. It was exchanged for that of Jubilee No 45632 *Tonga* (No 9149) which was transferred from Stockport Edgeley in August 1965 specifically for that purpose and then promptly withdrawn. The football stadium and floodlights are prominent beyond the carriage sidings, home of Blackpool FC who enjoyed a long period playing in the 1st Division - from pre-war days before being relegated at the end of 1966/67 season - just before the end of steam. **5TH JULY 1964 ● P. FITTON**

The long shadows of a large oak tree in full season extend almost to the permanent way in this idyllic late summer scene. Another old favourite, No **44933** in ex-works condition passes Salwick with the 11.15am Manchester Victoria to Blackpool North. Although showing Class A headlamps, the train has stopped at all stations via Bolton, excluding Salford and Salwick. **30TH AUGUST 1965 ● P. FITTON**

During the month of July 1963, the depot took delivery of no fewer than fourteen Class Fives. Some were seasonal transfers whilst others helped bolster an allocation which had recently lost members of the Patriot, Jubilee and Royal Scot classes. No **45118** was in the former category, having arrived from Carlisle Kingmoor for a three-month period. It had worked out of Perth in the early 1950's where a buffer beam snowplough was fitted but whether this was retained during its Kingmoor days and removed for the transfer remains unclear. Whilst at Newton Heath, the loco was naturally engaged on Blackpool duties and was caught bringing the afternoon 3.10pm from Manchester Victoria through Eastham, near Lytham, on the coast line towards Blackpool Central.

27TH JULY 1963 ● P. FITTON

When Belle Vue closed on 14th April 1956, Newton Heath were the recipient of an additional 16 locomotives. They were Nos 43756, 44022, 44119, 44486, 44803/45, 45031, 47440, 58128, 90122/6/40/2/97, 90316 and 90552. Two of the Class Fives, Nos **44803** and 44845 were seemingly inseparable and both survived until the depot's closure to steam on 1st July 1968. They were regularly rostered to work the 7am Manchester Victoria to Bradford Exchange parcels before running light engine to Leeds Central where they carried out the rare manoeuvre of traversing the line between Leeds 'B' box and Copley Hill in order to reach Farnley Junction shed. The engine later worked the 8.17pm Leeds to Stockport parcels. They both regularly featured on various football excursions and of course, took their turn on the Moston - Camden freights. On 6th October 1956, No 44803 was an unusual visitor at Edinburgh Princes Street but was caught on camera nearer home, storming through Bay Horse, between Garstang and Lancaster, with a Down parcels train.

18TH JULY 1964 ● E.F. BENTLEY

The 4.35pm Sundays Only Rochdale to Liverpool Exchange stopping train pauses at Castleton behind No **45154 Lanarkshire Yeomanry.** A little known fact about this engine is that it ran with a broken nameplate for a short period - the result of attempted theft which influenced the prompt removal of these increasingly desirable objects. It had been relegated exclusively to freight duties with a move to Aintree in January 1964 but, somewhat surprisingly, returned for a month in June 1964 before moving on yet again. Meanwhile No 45154 had been the Merseyside depot's first and last named locomotive. An interesting observation on 17th January 1963 was the Class Five caught working the 1.07pm Nottingham (Queens Walk) to Hotchley Hill trip along the ex-GCR main line.

30TH AUGUST 1959 ● R.S. GREENWOOD

A familiar vantage point on the ex-Midland Main line between Manchester Central and Derby was Chinley North Junction. One would normally expect to see a Trafford Park or Kentish Town Jubilee passing on a St. Pancras express here but on this occasion a southbound train from Blackpool North to Leicester is in the hands of No **44734.** Ex-LNER coaching stock often intermingled with LM and BR varieties on scratch sets such as this. The Class Five was one of a handful that spent the entire BR period at Newton Heath.

AUGUST 1963 ● **AUTHOR'S COLLECTION**

Further south, a troop train - Reporting Number C862, is from Manchester Victoria to Westbury and is recorded passing through Breadsall on the northern outskirts of Derby. The locomotive, No **44736** would probably have been relieved in the Birmingham area before the special proceeded via the Lickey Incline in the Bristol direction. The significance of letters 'AA' chalked on the smokebox door is unknown. Following the WW2, conscription was extended as peacetime National Service throughout the 1950's and such trains were commonplace. **9TH AUGUST 1953** ● **R.J. BUCKLEY**

The Royal Mail TPOs which arrived at Red Bank Carriage Sidings were normally turned on the Miles Platting triangle so as to be facing in the right direction for their next turn of work. On this occasion, the stock is making use of the Castleton triangle with Class Five No **44934** in attendance.

7TH JUNE 1966 ● R.S. GREENWOOD

Scarborough, that popular east coast resort, witnessed the arrival of numerous Newton Heath Crabs, Class Fives and Jubilees over the years with summer specials. Although the shed here closed as a steam depot on 20th May 1963, the turntable, coaling and watering facilities remained in situ and available for a further four years. Having brought in an excursion from Lancashire, No **45435** drifts on to a stabling road in the old shed yard which was overlooked by the Scarborough Town gas works complex.

22ND AUGUST 1966 ● J.A. PEDEN

Skirting around the side of the 'Parlour' at its home depot, No **45382** is technically 'at work', bringing a Cravens 2-Car Diesel Multiple Unit, seemingly out of commission, for stabling within the diesel depot. Above the fuel tanks in the foreground is the staff amenity block beyond which lies the Oldham branch. The boiler house, serving the diesel depot which opened in 1961, is visible above No 45382's tender whilst the 'Parlour' itself (the repair shop), parts of which date back to L&Y days, is behind the engine. The remaining 12 roads of the steam depot are out of view on the right but the coal hopper is just visible.

12TH MARCH 1966 ● P. JORDAN

A thunderous exhaust blackens the Gorton skies as Class Five No **44736** departs on Easter Bank Holiday Monday at 12.55pm with the empty stock of 1X42, a Leeds City to Belle Vue ADEX. The station was conveniently situated for the late and much lamented Belle Vue Zoological Gardens which attracted visitors from far and wide. This train would have arrived in the Manchester area by way of Huddersfield and Stalybridge and would then have traversed the freight only chord from Park Station to Ashburys via Midland Junction. The empty stock was stabled at Gowhole whilst the locomotive sought refreshment at Heaton Mersey. **11TH APRIL 1966 ● E.F. BENTLEY**

Another instance of their versatility occurred on Saturday, 17th January 1953 when Blackpool and Newton Heath MPDs provided the motive power for travelling supporters to the Midlands when West Bromwich Albion entertained Preston North End. Nos **44697** and 44737 (24E) went via Crewe, Market Drayton and Wellington. By 1966 such outings were but a memory as the loco passes through Guide Bridge Station light engine from Stockport (Edgeley).

1965 ● B. CRAMER

Taking the Chorley line at Dobbs Brow Junction is No 44934 with the 4.07 Manchester Victoria to Barrow express. The Dobbs Brow spur ran from the Atherton line to Blackrod, enabling trains not booked to call at Bolton to avoid the congestion there. A typical example of how 26A locos (particularly Class Fives) infiltrated other divisions occurred on 7th December 1950 when this loco was recorded hauling the 5.08pm Birmingham New Street to Leamington Spa via Berkswell and Kenilworth. It returned with the 8.25pm Leamington Spa - New Street.

c1955 ● W.D. COOPER

Blowing off in the still night air and with evidence of a dirty chimney, No **44933** waits to get away from Victoria's number 12 platform with the 8.55pm 'Belfast Boat Express', which had through coaches for Heysham. Arrival at the port was timetabled for 10.50pm with the connecting vessel scheduled for departure at 11.55pm, arriving in Belfast at 7.00am the following morning. It was unusual to find a Newton Heath engine on this working, which was normally handled by a Carnforth Jubilee or Class Five.

MARCH 1964 ● J. CLARKE

The Manchester Divisional Civil Engineer's Saloon, LMS M45045M is propelled by No **44818** past the remains of Atherton Bag Lane Station. The works inspection team are on their way to survey structures within the Bolton Great Moor Street Station vicinity prior to complete closure. The line from here to Kenyon Junction lost its passenger services as long ago as 27th March 1954 but Wakes Week specials destined for North Wales continued to make use of the route until the early 1960's.   **20TH SEPTEMBER 1966** ● **M. WELCH**

Ransome Rapier Crane RS 1083/45 returns to its Newton Heath base after having attended to repairs on the Pot Hall Rail Bridge at Heywood. Working tender first, No **44845** takes the rather unusual route via the Oldham Loop to get home. The breakdown train is between Shaw and Oldham on that exposed section of line that belies the close proximity of heavy industry. The 45 ton crane was transferred from Gorton MPD when it was closed in June 1965, by which time all lines west of Dunford Bridge came under LMR control. In 1981, break-down crane duties became the responsibility of Crewe and Springs Branch (Wigan) where 75 ton capacity cranes were located and RS 1083/45 was sold on to the Bluebell Railway, Sussex where it survives in preservation. On 21st April 1961, this ex Belle Vue locomotive passed through Aylesbury at 8.45pm on a Class D train comprising 41 vans from Brunswick (Liverpool) to Southampton (via Neasden and Feltham).   **4TH JULY 1966** ● **M. WELCH**

The last week of scheduled steam on the Manchester Victoria to Blackpool services was marked by Class Five No **45271** and other Newton Heath and Blackpool engines. Drawing alongside St. Mark's Road and passing Maudland Viaduct signal box on the Up Slow line, the crew observe the statutory 20mph restriction between here and Fylde Junction on the approaches to Preston Station.The train is the 12.40pm Blackpool Central to Manchester Victoria. **1ST SEPTEMBER 1964 ● P. FITTON**

One of the great train sheds in the country plays host to No **44736,** recently arrived at Preston's number 4 platform with a Blackpool extra. This was to be the last summer of steam and at least three other photographers are busy recording the happy scene. Meanwhile, a fair gathering of passengers await a main line arrival on neighbouring Platform 5, including a party of schoolboys venturing ever closer to the platform edge. A telegram service apparently in the waiting room remains available but this would soon be a memory, as would No 44736. **12TH AUGUST 1967 ● F.W. SHUTTLEWORTH**

Storming through New Hey Station with empty stock bound for Shaw to form a Blackpool excursion is No **45232**. Newton Heath drivers were generally considered masters of their craft and it was unusual to observe a dirty chimney from a locomotive on passenger work. Having been a 26A locomotive since LMS days, it was surprisingly reallocated to Burton MPD together with another diehard, No 45224 in May 1963.   **28TH MAY 1960 ● R.S. GREENWOOD**

York frequently witnessed the arrival of 26A locos, most of which brought a variety of freight and parcels traffic into the city. It was unusual to see No **44735** arriving from the east with the 4.03pm SO Filey/Scarborough to Newcastle train, an unbalanced working. The loco would be relieved here and make its way to York North MPD for servicing. The Operating Department would then either want it off shed, despatched in a homeward direction by the best means possible, or borrow it to fulfil its own needs if their own locos were in short supply. This particular engine enjoyed two spells on allocation. It sported a 26A shedplate as a long-standing resident from 1950 until 1964 but upon its return in March 1968, it had to be content with a stencilled 9D alternative. It arrived at a time when, ironically, four small Drewry diesel shunters (D2224/6/7/34) were withdrawn. 44735 had the distinction of being the last steam loco to work to the shed. It left on 29th June 1968 hauling 44809 bound for Carnforth and survived until the last day of steam.

10TH AUGUST 1963 ● P. FITTON

Deep in the heart of Pennine country, south of Todmorden lies Walsden - once in Lancashire but since 1888 firmly within the Yorkshire boundary. This idyllic view overlooking the south end of Winterbutlee tunnel sees No **44890** in charge of the SSO Scarborough to Liverpool Exchange service. The station, situated immediately north of the tunnel had closed in 1961 but local bus services remained and these were of more than a passing interest. The LMS had gained powers to operate motorbuses in the area under the 1928 Transport Act and as a result, Todmorden Corporation - established in 1907 - became Todmorden Corporation and Joint Omnibus Committee in 1931 with ownership of vehicles being equally divided. Fleet No **26** - a Leyland PD2/1 - passes by on the A6033 with the service from Todmorden to Summit. This was one of a batch of eight buses built in 1950 and, along with No 18, was owned by the Corporation. The other six were BR vehicles who had also inherited the LMS interest upon nationalisation. No 26 was withdrawn in 1969 at which time the National Bus Company had become the new owners. The abrupt valley from the cutting in the left foreground was the original route of the Rochdale Canal, diverted when the railway was built.

13TH JULY 1963 ● **I.G. HOLT**

The forerunner of the Class, a grimy No **45500** *Patriot* is caught in action north of the border ascending Beattock. The train is a Carlisle to Glasgow express with Kingmoor having borrowed the loco for a filling-in turn. It was unusual to find a 26A Patriot venturing north of Carlisle in BR days but in August 1934, the LMS sent two new members (after running in at Preston), Nos 5547 & 8 specifically to work the Manchester - Glasgow services throughout, augmented by Nos 5549/50 from Polmadie. They were replaced in 1943 by the Jubilees and Royal Scots (Polmadie only). **JULY 1960 ● AUTHOR'S COLLECTION**

THE PATRIOT 4-6-0's

South of Carlisle, again on the West Coast Main Line and No **45515** *Caernarvon* climbs towards Shap Summit unassisted and, despite its external condition, must have been in good mechanical order. It was perhaps significant that the following month, two other members, Nos 45539 *E.C. Trench* and 45509 *The Derbyshire Yeomanry* were both observed at Carlisle with the 9.15am Liverpool Exchange to Glasgow and the 2pm Manchester Victoria to Glasgow and Edinburgh respectively on 16th July. This, despite the fact that Newton Heath had Class 7P power available at that time. No 45515 was to become the last survivor of five unrebuilt examples which carried 26A shedplates and during a lifetime of nearly thirty years was coupled to no fewer than nine different tenders. In common with the majority of a class of 52 locos, it spent virtually all its time on the Western Division and arrived, surplus to requirements, from Edge Hill on 2nd April 1960. **25TH JUNE 1960 ● J. DAVENPORT**

Unrebuilt Patriot No 45509 _The Derbyshire Yeomanry_ was the second of the class to be allocated since the war, but was the shed's longest serving Patriot resident (August 1958 to withdrawal in August 1961). It was often diagrammed to work the intensive Blackpool residential services but, in common with the majority of Newton Heath's motive power, saw a great variety of work. It is seen here, passing the Dunlop Cotton Mills at Castleton with a Sunday excursion from Oldham Werneth to Blackpool. The train had been piloted around the Oldham Loop as far as Rochdale East Junction by Ivatt Class 2MT No 46484. **26TH JUNE 1960 ● R.S. GREENWOOD**

Having passed southbound through Preston Station with 1M21, the Glasgow - Blackpool (SO) express approaches Todd Lane Junction on the East Lancashire Line. The train will shortly branch west and pass Lostock Hall Station and MPD before regaining the northbound main line by way of Farington Curve Junction. Having competed this circuitous route, Rebuilt Patriot No **45522 _Prestatyn_** will then pass through Preston Station for a second time before taking the Blackpool line at Maudland Junction, much to the confusion of many travelling Glaswegians! **AUGUST 1962 ● W. ASHCROFT**

Rebuilt Patriot No 45522 _Prestatyn_ was the only one of its type to be allocated. It came north from Kentish Town with four Royal Scots (see page 95) in September 1961, all of which had been made redundant by the arrival of the Type 4 'Peak' diesels. Leaving Pendleton in its wake and passing Irlam Signalbox, No 45522 is opening up to begin the assault on Pendlebury Bank with a Southport express. Rather surprisingly, it moved over the city to Longsight (with No 46142 _The York and Lancaster Regiment_) in June 1963 as the depot were short of power for summer extras. It then worked out of Trafford Park (unofficially) and featured regularly on the 5.22pm commuter train to Buxton for a short period. Withdrawn in September 1964, _Prestatyn_ languished at Buxton MPD until bought by The Central Wagon Co. in April 1965.

12TH JULY 1962 ● W.D. COOPER

With the sun setting over the Irish Sea, the pioneer - No **45500 _Patriot_** departs from Blackpool Central with a returning Yorkshire bound excursion. This may be a Todmorden train as Newton Heath handled most traffic originating from that town, otherwise it would have been borrowed. A Fleetwood 'Crab' 2-6-0 No **42841** and a Mirfield 8F No **48076** stand coupled together behind the train waiting to set back on to later departures. The centre bosses of the original Claughton wheels which were retained on _Patriot_ are nicely highlighted from this high vantage point overlooking the throat of the station. **18TH JUNE 1960 ● P. FITTON**

Climbing the 1 in 94 west of Bury and about to pass the local Grammar School playing fields is 4-6-0 No **45539 *E.C. Trench*.** A heavy exhaust lingers from the 6.5pm Rochdale to Hellifield fitted freight between the aptly named Bridge Road overbridge and the metal span carrying the lines which serve Bolton Street Station some 100 yards distant. The Patriots (other than No 45503 *The Royal Leicestershire Regiment*) were occasional performers on this train but the motive power was more likely to be a Class Five or a Crab.

7TH AUGUST 1961 ● **E.F. BENTLEY**

▲

After being kept standing in the Up main platform at Bolton Trinity Street, the signalman at Bolton East Junction box has eventually offered the road to No **45509 *The Derbyshire Yeomanry*.** The train is the 10.15am from Fleetwood/Blackpool to Manchester Victoria - note the fish van behind the tender. Approaching on the through road, having passed under Orlando Bridge, is WD 2-8-0 No **90264**, a long-time Rose Grove engine with a variety of open wagons.

10TH JUNE 1959 ● **B.W.B. BROOKSBANK**

No 45539 *E.C. Trench* once more, but more appropriately ▶ on summer seasonal work. The train has stopped to pick up passengers in the Wigan platform at Lostock Junction, having left Bolton Trinity Street with a North Wales Holiday Special. It will reverse at Wigan, probably involving a change of engine. In previous years, traffic between the Lancashire town and North Wales would have used Great Moor Street Station offering the more direct route via Kenyon Junction, Earlestown & Winwick Junction and usually involving Patricroft locomotives.

24TH JUNE 1961 ● **E.F. BENTLEY**

Class Fives, Jubilees and Crabs are the classes of loco usually associated with straying far off the beaten path. When No **45515** ***Caernarvon*** was discovered in the Neath roundhouse on 19th February 1961, it caused a mild sensation amongst the spotting fraternity deep in South Wales. It had apparently failed whilst working the previous day's 7.55pm Cardiff to Swansea parcels and was taken off at Neath. The train was rostered for a Shrewsbury engine on Saturdays only and Salop had obviously borrowed the loco. *Caernarvon* remained at Neath until 1st March because of a difficulty in obtaining spares. The loco is very much on home ground when seen leaving Kirkham with a dirty chimney and the 3.10pm Manchester Victoria to Blackpool Central via the coast line. Its condition remained dire until withdrawal on 9th June 1962 when it was placed in store at the rear of Bolton shed prior to cutting up at Crewe Works.

10TH SEPTEMBER 1960 ● P. FITTON

Hughes/Fowler 2-6-0 No 42700, Fowler rebuild 4-6-0 No 45500 *Patriot* and BR Standard 4-6-2 No 70000 *Britannia* were all forerunners of their class but had one other thing in common. All three had spells on allocation at Newton Heath during the BR period and two survive in preservation. What a pity that No **45500** ***Patriot*** did not complete the set, especially considering its prototype historical connections and the significance of a name eventually passed on from Claughton No 5964, withdrawn in July 1934. *PATRIOT In memory of fallen LNWR employees 1914 - 1919* was the wording carried by both locomotives. No 45500 is on a regular duty, passing Bradkirk signalbox with the 2.50pm Manchester Victoria to Blackpool North train.

4TH SEPTEMBER 1960 ● P. FITTON

Passing through the platforms at Blackrod with the 4.07pm Manchester Victoria to Barrow express is No **45509 The Derbyshire Yeomanry,** a regular performer on this job. The empty stock for the 'Barrer' was stabled at Lightbowne Sidings, opposite the shed and for whatever reason, the pilot (usually a Fowler 2-6-2T) would usually draw out the roofboarded carriages on to the headshunt as early as 2.15pm. This happened in full view of the crew who would be about to commence preparing their locomotive. Owing to poor patronage, the timetable was revised in later years and the rear portion was detached at Preston for Blackpool North. No 45509 was unique during the war years, in so far as it was the only Patriot known to have suffered any damage from enemy action. This was at Willesden in October 1940 whilst on allocation there. A two month sojourn at Crewe put matters to rights.

8TH JULY 1960 ● D. HAMPSON

The conditions were far from ideal. The going was damp at Dowbridge, near Kirkham but the poor weather did not deter the drivers of their respective engines, Nos **45515 Caernarvon** (1J29) on the Up Fast and Class Five No **45318** (1J64) on the Up Slow from taking up the challenge. Such a situation often occurred on a busy summer Saturday when, at certain times of the day, trains between Preston and Kirkham passed by every few minutes. At least the race kept the younger element of the travelling public entertained for a while. Both locos were regular performers - No 45318 was a long standing Blackpool engine which survived on allocation until September 1964 when it moved on to Bury. Blackpool Central station and south shed closed on 2nd November 1964.

1ST JULY 1961 ● P. FITTON

About to draw to a stand in Platform 5 at Preston Station is the 4.15pm Manchester Exchange to Glasgow Central with **No 45539 E.C. Trench** at its head. A stop of five minutes was allowed for the loading of parcels etc but the odd knowledgeable passenger might pay a quick visit to the legendary buffet, situated at the south end of Platforms 5 and 6. It was from here that hundreds of Preston's townsfolk gave of their time to keep the Buffet open, both day and night, from the commencement of the war in 1939. They supplied free refreshment to the millions of men and women of the fighting forces who passed through the station, either by the willing band of helpers at the carriage windows or in the buffet itself. Despite the fact that crockery was clearly marked 'Please return to Preston Station. Free Buffet for H.M. Forces', cups taken away by servicemen were known to have turned up in the United States, Africa, India and Italy.

11TH JUNE 1960 ● W.A. BROWN

During its short stay, No **45503** *The Royal Leicestershire Regiment* worked on the Scotswood to Red Bank empty vans on a number of occasions, both as pilot and train engine. The Patriot had the company of Class Five No **45076** when seen passing through Castleton but the previous day had piloted Crab 2-6-0 No 42707.   **10TH SEPTEMBER 1958 ● R.S. GREENWOOD**

This unrebuilt Patriot was the first to arrive during the BR period, albeit for only a short while. It came from Crewe North on 26th July 1958, presumably to assist over the remainder of the summer timetable, as it returned to 5A ten weeks later. Clearly showing its 26A shedplate, No **45503** *The Royal Leicestershire Regiment* awaits departure from the west end of Platform 14 at Manchester Victoria with an excursion train.

AUGUST 1958 ● W. A. BROWN

Emerging from the shadowy depths of Number 16 platform at Manchester Victoria Station is No **45500** *Patriot.* The train was from Southport but the lamps have been repositioned indicating empty stock to Red Bank, after which the loco will go light engine to Newton Heath shed. Photographer Gordon Coltas enjoyed many hours on the platforms here recording everyday scenes such as this. The arrival of the forerunner of the class was an added bonus as the unrebuilt Patriots were, without doubt, his favourite class of engine - with the Jubilees coming a close second!

28TH MAY 1960 ● G. COLTAS

The 8.05am Carlisle to Hellifield slow consisting of three different coaches (the first of which is corridor stock) and a parcels van, calls at the picturesque Horton in Ribblesdale station. The return working of the 11.58am from Hellifield needed ample power, for as many as 9 loaded milk tanks might be attached at Appleby, hence the presence of No **45522 Prestatyn.** The tanks went forward from Carlisle as part of the 4.30pm milk to Willesden.

27TH JULY 1962 ● R. JOANES

No 45509 *The Derbyshire Yeomanry* ▶ calls at Ansdell with the 3.10pm from Manchester Victoria to Blackpool Central.

15TH JUNE 1960 ● P. FITTON

◀ **A lightweight Bolton to Royton Junction freight** passes through Castleton on a rather miserable day behind No **45539 E.C. Trench,** running without a shedplate. The locomotive initially arrived on loan from Carnforth on 26th March 1960 but the transfer became official seven days after this photograph was taken.

18TH MAY 1960 ● R.S. GREENWOOD

THE JUBILEE CLASS 4-6-0's

Newton Heath MPD were the recipients of eight new Jubilees, delivered ex-works from Crewe between 23rd March and 5th May 1936. Nos 5695 - 5702 spent varying periods at the depot with No 5697 *Achilles* moving straight on to Blackpool after running in. No 5700 *Britannia*, later renamed *Amethyst (see below)* spent virtually all its life there, working mainly over the Central Division. No **45700 Amethyst** breasts the summit at Shap with a southbound train from Carlisle to Manchester Victoria.   **17TH AUGUST 1960 ● R. FARRELL**

No 45700 AMETHYST

When BR Standard Pacific No 70000 *Britannia* was unveiled in February 1951, No 45700 immediately lost its nameplates. The loco ran nameless for seven months until receiving the new name *Amethyst*, which had been suggested by members of the Railway Correspondence and Travel Society (RCTS). Apparently it carried a chalked inscription *Farouk* for short while. On Summer Saturdays the Jubilees could be seen far and wide and on this occasion No **45700 Amethyst** is drawing out of the platforms at Stafford with a Crewe bound train.   **8TH AUGUST 1956 ● B. MORRISON**

A Jubilee in full cry was always a most impressive sight. Another outing over the West Coast Main Line sees No **45700** *Amethyst* bearing down on the cameraman - having topped up its Fowler tender on Hademore Troughs (situated two miles south of Lichfield). The train is the 9.45am (SO) Blackpool Central to London Euston (W330) and the loco has been borrowed by 24E.

AUGUST 1960 ● G. COLTAS

The driver gives a wave as his engine, Jubilee No **45700** and temporarily unnamed, works a lightweight Manchester Exchange to Leeds express near Diggle. Fowler tender No 3913, which was paired with the loco throughout the LMS period, now bears the short lived inscription BRITISH RAILWAYS.

JULY 1951 ● J. DAVENPORT

Easing its way on to the West Coast Main Line is No **45700** *Britannia* at Morecambe South Junction with the 2.30pm Morecambe - London Euston express. This was unusual motive power and, being a summer Sunday, *Britannia* may well have worked 'W66' throughout to the capital. Towards the end of the 1957 Summer Timetable, this engine 'bucked a trend' which was to follow in later years. The Newton Heath Operating Department obviously considered they had sufficient serviceable locomotives to hand as it went to Blackpool on 7th September for a three week period. This was to cover for their own Jubilees, Nos 45580 *Burma* and 45584 *North West Frontier* which were both away at Crewe receiving attention.

20TH AUGUST 1950 ● I.S. PEARSALL

No 45737 ATLAS

One of the saddest spectacles towards the end of steam was to witness once proud express locos relegated to mundane duties. Such was the case here at Gowhole where No **45737** *Atlas* is being turned having arrived with a freight from Moston Exchange Sidings. In days of old, Jubilees were regularly seen here of course, pounding away on the Midland main line between Manchester Central and London St. Pancras - but rarely within the goods yards. Four other locos are present, indicating the volume of traffic still handled at this remote outpost. A B1 4-6-0 slinks by with mineral wagons whilst another is just visible behind the named Class Five (either No 45154 *Lanarkshire Yeomanry* or No 45156 *Ayrshire Yeomanry*). Another un-named member stands alongside the water pylon. **AUGUST 1962** ● **AUTHOR'S COLLECTION**

No 45679 ARMADA

Reporting Number C453 indicated the 3.30pm Blackpool North - Cleethorpes and the train is seen here bowling along in fine style at Bradkirk behind No **45679** *Armada* - the summer season nearly over. **3RD SEPTEMBER 1960** ● **P. FITTON**

One of the few Jubilees to retain a smaller, 3,500 gallon Fowler tender until withdrawal was this example. No **45679** *Armada* is again employed on holiday traffic from the Fylde coast and is entering the platforms at Preston Station where LNWR pattern restricted visibility semaphore signals still co-exist alongside the colour light variety. Whilst at 26A, *Armada* could be regularly found on the Rowsley turns but is perhaps unique in having been repaired at four different workshops. This much travelled engine began life on the Western Division (1935-40), then moved to the Midland (1940-52), on to the Scottish Region (1952-59), back to the Western Division (1959/60) and finally the Central Division (1960-62). Records show that it passed through Crewe, Derby, St. Rollox and Cowlairs Works at various periods.

AUGUST 1962 ● **B.W.L. BROOKSBANK**

The departure of Nos 45600 *Bermuda* and 45593 *Kolhapur* from the former LNWR depot at Patricroft in January 1965 was significant. It ended their association with the Jubilee class and a number of the older drivers found it particularly galling that *Bermuda* was to go up the road to the Lanky. *Kolhapur* had recently arrived from Burton and was held in less esteem, whereas No 45600 had been the pride of the shed since June 1950. It came as little surprise that both locos' conditions were dire on arrival but No 45593 was soon on the move again - to Leeds Holbeck from where it gained a high profile which eventually resulted in preservation. *Bermuda,* on the other hand, soldiered on throughout the year doing whatever work that could be made available. Caught in deep shadow, No 45600 is passing through Marple Station with a Permanent Way train bound for Gowhole.

9TH OCTOBER 1965 ● P. FITTON

No 45600 BERMUDA

An unlikely location to find a Newton Heath Jubilee was under the wires at Manchester Piccadilly Station. After the modernisation scheme of 1960, steam remained in sporadic evidence there until such time as it was banished from Longsight on 14th February 1965 followed by the closure of nearby Gorton MPD four months later. After this, their presence became a rarity but No **45600** *Bermuda* stands in a rather deserted station polluting the atmosphere whilst awaiting departure with empty stock. The train comprising six non corridor carriages hard up against the buffers was as rare a sight as the loco by this time.

AUGUST 1965 ● J. CLARKE

With wheezing steam escaping from its cylinders, the 9.00am to Glasgow Central blasts away from Victoria's Platform 11 Middle and on through Manchester Exchange leaving a trail of exhaust swirling in its wake under the train shed roof. The loco pressed into service is No **45600** *Bermuda* which would doubtless require assistance on the climb to Shap, but would be relieved at Carlisle. This was probably its final fling over a route to which it was well accustomed. Patricroft had regular fast freight and newspaper workings to the city and *Bermuda* featured prominently on these turns in years gone by.

6TH MARCH 1965 ● G. COLTAS

A westbound steel train comes off the 'new line' at Manchester Victoria East Junction on a bright Wednesday morning at 10.00am behind No **45600 Bermuda.** By this time the loco had lost its nameplates and unfortunately remained in this woebegone condition until withdrawal. Meanwhile Stanier 2-6-4T No **42656** is at work shunting parcels vans. This particular loco arrived from Bolton in June 1964 before returning there 26 months later! Notice the cleaned outline only of the totem on the tank side.   **21ST APRIL 1965** ● **P. FITTON**

No 45642 BOSCAWEN

A long-standing resident was Jubilee 4-6-0 No 45642 Boscawen. This loco was the original forerunner of the class having been built at Crewe in May 1934 as No 5552 and at first un-named. After a later engine, No 5642, was built at Crewe in December 1934 (also initially un-named), it was decided to give the latter engine the number 5552 and name it *Silver Jubilee*, this being done in April 1935. The original No 5552 was then renumbered No 5642 and named *Boscawen* in April 1936. It was considered by many Newton Heath men to be the 'black sheep' of the family, possibly because it was the forerunner of the class and retained certain dubious prototype features. It had nevertheless managed to reach the summit of Miles Platting incline with a Leeds bound express, no doubt with the assistance of a banking engine. Notice the gradient post: 1 in 48, 1 in 160. Meanwhile a Fowler 4F 0-6-0 reverses over the main line from New Allen Street Junction and will pass through Brewery Sidings en route to the shed for servicing.   **1950** ● **A. BENDELL**

Hanslope, north of Castlethorpe, was one of the more remote locations on the West Coast Main Line, situated on the section between Wolverton and Roade. On a summer Saturday in 1954, two northbound relief trains passed within a short time of each other, each hauled by a Newton Heath Jubilee. The first, with No 45702 *Colossus* in charge, appears on page 70. The second was this special from Portsmouth, Reporting Number W683 and destined for Oldham Mumps, as was the first train. The driver of No **45642 Boscawen** has acknowledged Peter Hutchinson's presence by the lineside. After unloading at Mumps Station, both locos were originally diagrammed to take their stock to Lightbowne Sidings, arriving at 9.27pm and 9.55pm respectively. However a supplement to the special traffic notice stated that the stock of W681, hauled by *Colossus,* was to be left at Morley.

26TH JUNE 1954 ● P. HUTCHINSON

Awaiting the signal for Red Bank Carriage Sidings after an arrival at Manchester Victoria from Blackpool is filthy No **45642 Boscawen.** The Stanier tender coupled to the loco was that which was previously attached to 8F No 48506. The pair came together on 25th January 1959 and remained united until withdrawal during the first week of January 1965 - surprisingly late in the day, considering the engine's poor reputation. In happier days, it was one of three 26A Jubilees (the others being Nos 45635 *Tobago* and 45701 *Conqueror*) amongst 36 engines which travelled to London in connection with the 1953 FA Cup Final at Wembley between Blackpool and Bolton Wanderers.

10TH JULY 1964 ● G. COLTAS

A three-coach slow passenger train on the West Coast Main Line was hardly a regular working for No **45642 Boscawen.** The original forerunner of the class is well off its beaten track, caught running into Norton Bridge Station's Down Fast platform. A possible explanation might have been a visit to Crewe Works followed by a running in turn - but according to records this wasn't the case and the loco is hardly in ex-works condition anyway. A southbound express disappears into the distance having passed *Boscawen* at speed.

3rd JULY 1954 ● E. R. MORTEN

A classic location on the approach to Ais Gill Summit. With Wild Boar Fell in the background, Jubilee 4-6-0 No **45601** *British Guiana* brings a Heads of Ayr to Leeds train through the Mallerstang Valley. It was unusual to find a 26A engine on this duty - presumably either Carlisle Kingmoor or Leeds Holbeck had borrowed the loco.   **24TH AUGUST 1963** ● **D. CASH**

No 45601 BRITISH GUIANA

Having left Crewe Works after receiving its last Heavy General Overhaul some three weeks previously, No **45601** *British Guiana* remained commendably clean when caught passing Kirkham working the 10.35am Manchester Victoria to Blackpool North/Fleetwood train which ran separately throughout from the Blackpool Central portion. During its six week stay at Crewe, *British Guiana* was fitted with a speedometer and lasted in service at 26A for a further three years, surviving a period of storage at the end of 1962. The condition of both rolling stock and mineral wagon nicely complement the loco.   **14TH OCTOBER 1961** ● **P. FITTON**

Approaching Shotton Station with the 7.40am Manchester Exchange to Caernarfon (1D04) is No **45602 British Honduras.** The Jubilee was one of at least four Newton Heath engines observed on the North Wales coast line later that day. Class Five No 45101 worked 1Z31 Cheadle (Staffs) to Llandudno Relief and passed through Connahs Quay at 9.00am - six minutes ahead of schedule - followed by British Honduras on the Down Fast 20 minutes later. At 11.38am, Class Five No 44696 appeared with the 9.06am Birmingham New Street to Holyhead (1D32) closely followed by No 44736 on the 10.20am Manchester Exchange to Llandudno (1D35). No 45602 returned, rather surprisingly, with the 12.30pm Llandudno to Leeds City (1N86 via Stockport Edgeley) as did No 44736 with the 3.14pm Llandudno to Manchester Exchange Relief (1C85).

4TH AUGUST 1962 ● R. JOANES

No 45602 BRITISH HONDURAS

A turn which was regularly diagrammed for a Jubilee was the 8.00am from Colne to London Euston as far as Stockport Edgeley. No **45602 British Honduras** stands in the 'slums', having already detached from the three through carriages destined for London Euston. The engine crew and passengers await the arrival of the main train, the 10.10am from Manchester Piccadilly which will arrive in four minutes time according to the clock on Platform 3. Six minutes are then allowed for the Edgeley pilot (usually a Fowler 2-6-4T) to marshal these coaches on to the rear. After departure at 10.25am, No 45602 would proceed to Edgeley shed for servicing - the lamp having already been set. The 'Jubs' were also regularly observed on the Scotswood - Red Bank empty newspaper vans and doing duty on 12th June 1962 were British Honduras piloting its old shedmate No 45685 Barfleur (82E). Before arriving at 26A from Canklow on 3rd March 1962, No 45602 had been a long standing Midland Division engine with spells at Bristol (Barrow Road) during the 1950's.

17TH MARCH 1962 ● G. WHITEHEAD

No 45604 CEYLON

Empty stock from Cheetham Hill Carriage Sidings passes beneath Cheetham Hill Road bridge and into Platform 14 at Manchester Victoria Station. It will form the 1.05pm Fridays Only express to Glasgow and is hauled by No **45604 Ceylon** as far as Carlisle. This Jubilee was hardly associated with the shed, spending only its final three months in service before withdrawal in July 1965. It had primarily been a Western Division locomotive but spent the war years and up to 1951 at Leeds Holbeck.

18TH JUNE 1965 ● M.S. STOKES

The upper valley of the Lune is an area of outstanding natural beauty within which are situated Dillicar Troughs, one mile south of Tebay Station. No **45702 *Colossus*** picks up water, racing southbound with a modest load of only seven bogies. The troughs here were renewed as late as 1961 despite impending dieselisation. **4TH AUGUST 1960 ● G. COLTAS**

No 45702 COLOSSUS

Passing through Leeds City with the Scotswood to Red Bank empty vans is No **45702 *Colossus*** piloting shedmate Class Five No **45224**. Although the photograph is undated, this combination worked the train on a number of occasions according to the records.

c1958 ● AUTHOR'S COLLECTION

Another day out to London for No **45702 *Colossus*.** The Jubilee returns home through Lichfield Trent Valley Station with a summer Saturday excursion whilst a local passenger service to Birmingham New Street is ready to depart from the City Station behind Fowler 2-6-4T No **42422** (Monument Lane) working bunker first. *Colossus* was the last of the batch (Nos 5695 -5702) sent new to Newton Heath. It left for Southport in 1938 but after a succession of depots it returned in December 1950 where it stayed until withdrawal.

30TH JULY 1955 ● D.J. MONTGOMERY

No 45702 *Colossus* passes through Hanslope with a returning excursion *(see page 68)*. Despite having a Fowler tender until February 1959, it handled a fair share of Glasgow turns, occasionally requiring assistance either side of Carlisle, but on 27th June 1952 the 10.45am from Glasgow arrived at Manchester Victoria with ex-L&Y 2-4-2T No 50852 (Lostock Hall) piloting the ailing Jubilee. On the occasion of 19th November 1956, it worked the 2.10pm Carlisle to Glasgow Central instead of the usual 66A *Britannia* or *Royal Scot,* returning south next day with the 10.55am Glasgow to Manchester and Liverpool, loaded to 15 bogies which came into Carlisle 6 minutes late with No 44952 (64D) as pilot. This was detached in favour of No 40692 (12A). A further observation on 2nd June 1957 saw the inaugural 6.38pm twice weekly 'car sleeper' from Glasgow St Enoch to London Marylebone, made up to eleven vehicles, leaving behind No 45702, as Corkerhill were apparently unable to provide one of their own engines.

26TH JUNE 1954 ● P. HUTCHINSON

No 45701 CONQUEROR

Approaching Droylsden with a Manchester Exchange to Leeds semi-fast is No 45701 *Conqueror*. This was the Jubilee which shared the distinction alongside Leeds Holbeck's Nos 45658 *Keyes* and 45659 *Drake* of spending an entire lifetime at one depot.

JULY 1960 ● J. DAVENPORT

The Coronation Day of 1953 found No **45701 *Conqueror*** on a Glasgow turn. Driver Billy Higgins and Fireman Bob Hamilton were one of eight such Driver/Fireman teams which comprised the Glasgow Link. Both had both lodged at Polmadie overnight and are fit and raring to go with the 10.15am departure from Glasgow Central. Fireman Hamilton was on his first trip north of the border and although the work was hard, he would appreciate the high mileage bonuses. A driver in this link in the mid 1950s could expect to earn about £10.12s a week, supplemented by an average £4 mileage allowance.

2ND JUNE 1953 ● AUTHOR'S COLLECTION

No 45701 *Conqueror* comes off the north end of Dillicar Troughs with the 9.43 (SO) Liverpool Exchange to Glasgow Central and Edinburgh Princes Street. Although Jubilees regularly reached Glasgow from Manchester coupled to 3,500 gallon tenders, on 17th July 1956 No 45701 came off at Carlisle with the 4.15pm ex Manchester because of insufficient coal in the tender to complete the journey. No 46222 *Queen Mary* (66A) took over, this being one of the few instances of a Duchess in use on a Manchester - Glasgow working. After replenishment at Kingmoor, No 45701 went forward from Carlisle with the 7.50pm to Glasgow St. Enoch via the G&SW route. Whether the Newton Heath crew stayed with their Jubilee or manned the Pacific went unrecorded.   **14TH JUNE 1958** ● **B. HILTON**

***Conqueror* was renumbered 45701** week ending 22nd May 1948 and carried a serif style front numberplate for a short period. The loco is entering Crewe Station from the south clearly displaying the numerals. Two other Jubilees, Nos 45571 *India* and 45584 *North West Frontier*, both of Blackpool MPD were on Newton Heath shed in immaculate condition, having been prepared to work the Royal Train on the occasion of the visit by Her Majesty to South Lancashire in 1954. No 45701 *Conqueror* was detailed as the standby engine on the day.

25TH JUNE 1949 ● **T. LEWIS**

No 45701 Conqueror appears to have plenty of coal in its tender on this occasion and is back at Carlisle Citadel Station after servicing at Kingmoor MPD. It had arrived earlier in the day with a Glasgow express and will await a return working in the centre road, possibly as a pilot loco.

JUNE 1961 ● **D. YOUNG COLLECTION**

No 45711 COURAGEOUS

The one that got away. Having spent the greater part of World War 2 and the immediate post war years at 26A, *Courageous* moved on to 'Wessie' territory on 4th September 1948, taking up residence at Farnley Junction. Four years later it moved north of the border to Glasgow, never to return, alternating between Corkerhill and Polmadie MPD's. It became a rare bird to the spotting fraternity although it paid at least one visit to Manchester on 17th November 1960 where it was observed on Newton Heath sporting a 67A shedplate - a stranger indeed! This photo just qualifies for the book as it was taken at Manchester Victoria Station barely three months after Nationalisation and No **5711 *Courageous*** has yet to receive its BR number. Also of interest is that during the LMS period, it was the only Jubilee ever to be allocated to Accrington MPD. (18th June 1938 - 5th November 1938).

13TH MARCH 1948 ● H.C. CASSERLEY

No 45706 EXPRESS

With through coaches from London Euston, the 2.29pm (Saturdays Only) Manchester Victoria to Colne blasts through the remains of Turton and Edgworth Station (which had closed to passengers some seven months earlier) and up the bank towards Entwistle. No **45706 *Express*** is in charge and is on time, passing at 3.05pm. A lone figure standing on a badly crumbling brick platform witnesses its passage. Although the station building had recently suffered from the ravages of fire, the withered remnants of a hanging basket survive, suggesting that the staff once took a pride in the place. The goods yard lingered on until the end of 1964. **9TH SEPTEMBER 1961 ● E. BENTLEY**

On leaving Blackburn on the Bolton line, trains were faced with a continual climb of just over seven miles, the final 2,015 yards of which were through the damp and inhospitable Sough Tunnel. The crew of No **45706** *Express* no doubt welcomed a breath of fresh air having just cleared the tunnel and reached the summit at Waltons Sidings. The 8am Colne - London Euston through service was a regular Jubilee turn which worked as far as Stockport Edgeley. Visible are the gradient post indicating 1 in 72 in each direction whilst the retaining wall formed part of a channel diverting a brook away from the railway.

18TH AUGUST 1962 ● D. HAMPSON

No **45706** *Express* takes the through line at Skew Bridge with a Blackpool excursion. This will avoid passing through the platforms at Preston Station. Note the ex-LMS Stanier articulated corridor coaches forming the train.

c1956 ● A. HAYNES COLLECTION

As their front-line locomotives for many years, Newton Heath's Jubilees were always kept in excellent mechanical condition by the chargehand fitters there. Unfortunately their external condition often left much to be desired and a well groomed 26A loco at work usually meant it was ex-works. On Easter Monday 1956, it came as a pleasant surprise to record No **45706** *Express* immaculately turned out for a Marsden to Scarborough excursion. The train is passing through the northern outskirts of Leeds at Cross Gates and the distinctive nameplate (which incorporated a plaque beneath the raised plate which depicted Mercury, the winged messenger), adorning the front splasher is clearly visible.

2ND APRIL 1956 ● B.K.B. GREEN

No 45719 GLORIOUS

Storming up Miles Platting bank with an express passenger working over the former LNWR route to Leeds is No **45719** *Glorious*. This locomotive is perhaps better remembered in the BR period for passing Newton Heath whilst working over the Calder Valley main line on Liverpool Exchange to Newcastle trains as far as York. After transfer to Bank Hall in March 1953, it was a regular performer alongside Nos 45698 *Mars* and 45717 *Dauntless*, both also former 26A locos. It spent a nine month sojourn at Blackpool from September 1954 before returning to Merseyside, during which time it regularly visited its old haunts for servicing off the residentials. Whilst at 26A, the locomen nicknamed it *'Gormless'*, perhaps in reference to its condition at the time.

c.1950 ● A. BENDELL

The SO Blackpool North to Leicester (M336) races through Dowbridge, between Kirkham and Salwick, on the Up Fast behind No **45652 *Hawke*.** Once clear of Preston, the train will, in all probability, take the Whelley loop and on to Glazebrook before traversing the CLC to Cheadle Heath. As a former Trafford Park, Leicester and Kentish Town loco, *Hawke* will then be on familiar ground for the remainder of the journey. The following train, which appeared minutes later, was a Blackpool Central to Perth extra hauled by the next numerical Jubilee, No 45653 *Barham* from Blackpool MPD. **16TH JULY 1960 ● P. FITTON**

No 45652 HAWKE

The 1.30pm Manchester Victoria to Carlisle, first introduced in October 1955, became an additional Newton Heath working. Originally, the engine went on to Kingmoor after arrival at Carlisle and returned overnight with the Fraserburgh to Manchester fish via Hellifield. On Fridays the train ran through to Glasgow and as the fish train did not run on Friday nights, the engine was then diagrammed to return on the Sunday 11.55pm Glasgow Central to Manchester Exchange, but - being at the mercy of Polmadie in the meantime, that was not always the case. No **45652 *Hawke*** awaits departure with the train from Manchester Victoria.

6TH JUNE 1963 ● G. COLTAS

No 45652 Hawke's stay coincided with the transitional period when English Electric Type 4's eventually ousted the Jubilees on the Glasgow turns. Nevertheless, it reached Scotland on a number of occasions and in common with the other Jubilees, had notable trips. On June 7th 1960, whilst still on loan, the combined Liverpool and Manchester portions of the 10.50am from Glasgow made a load of 15 bogies. No 45652 was piloted as far as Carlisle by 45728 *Defiance* (12B) and No 45270 (5A) from there. On 1st March 1961, the same train arrived at Carlisle with a Kingmoor Class Five as pilot which was replaced by a Kingmoor Pacific, No 46226 *Duchess of Norfolk* - a far cry indeed from the Class 2P 4-4-0s of three years earlier. *Hawke* is performing more mundane duties at Low Moor with the 8.55am Manchester to Leeds stopping train.

17TH SEPTEMBER 1961 ● G. COLTAS

No 45654 HOOD

The withdrawal from service of No 45654 *Hood* in the week ending 25th June 1966 ended Newton Heath's association with the Jubilee class which had lasted over 30 years. First to arrive had been LMS No 5591 (later named Udaipur) from Edge Hill on 30th March 1935, to be followed by no fewer than forty six other members allocated over different periods. This total included the delivery of a new batch from Crewe Works, Nos 5695 - 5702 between 28th March and 9th May 1936. For No 5701 *Conqueror* it was the only move, remaining at 26A throughout its lifetime. No 45654 *Hood*, kept in a presentable condition, gets away from Preston under Fishergate Bridge and makes for the Fylde coast. A regular night turn for the engine earlier in the year had been the 'Blackpool Papers'

APRIL 1966 ● G. HARROP

The BR summer timetables invariably placed a great strain on Newton Heath's resources, especially with all the extra excursion traffic in connection with annual holidays from towns around the northern fringes of Manchester. Over the years the Operating Department had gained a notorious reputation for stopping larger visiting locomotives which arrived on shed during the week preceding a 'Wakes Weekend'. Whatever the reason given, they were miraculously available come Saturday! The situation would become even more desperate with the onset of the 1961 timetable because of the non-availability of several of their own Jubilees.

Of the eleven allocated, No 45661 *Vernon*, probably the best performer at the time, was already away at Crewe receiving a Heavy General Overhaul. No 45679 *Armada* (a former Carlisle Kingmoor engine) was about to be despatched to St. Rollox for a Light Intermediate followed by Nos 45601 *British Guiana* (Heavy General - Crewe) and 45700 *Amethyst* (Light Intermediate - Crewe). No 45635 *Tobago* was running rough and due for overhaul whilst No 45642 *Boscawen* had always been poorly regarded. On the plus side, Nos 45652 *Hawke*, 45701 *Conqueror*, 45702 *Colossus*, 45706 *Express* and 45710 *Irresistible* had all been through shops earlier in the year and were in fine working order. Control deemed that certain members of the class from the Midland Division could be made temporarily available to cover over the holiday period. The recent introduction of large numbers of 'Peak' Type 4 diesels on the ex-Midland main lines resulted in some being surplus to requirements. The transfer to the Central Division involved seven locomotives as follows:

	ARRIVED	HOME DEPOT	RETURNED
No **45585** *Hyderabad*	1st July 1961	Leicester (Midland)	23rd September 1961
No **45615** *Malay States*	8th July 1961	Leicester (Midland)	23rd September 1961
No **45622** *Nyasaland*	1st July 1961	Kentish Town	15th July 1961
No **45628** *Somaliland*	15th July 1961	Kentish Town	23rd September 1961
No **45636** *Uganda*	1st July 1961	Leicester (Midland)	23rd September 1961
No **45650** *Blake*	1st July 1961	Leicester (Midland)	26th August 1961
No **45712** *Victory*	1st July 1961	Kentish Town	23rd September 1961

Enjoying a summer sabbatical on the Central Division, No 45585 *Hyderabad* passes through Preston Station with a southbound excursion composed of non-corridor stock. This loco had previously been selected by Kentish Town MPD for high speed trials between London St. Pancras and Manchester Central (August 25/26th 1959) in conjunction with the impending introduction of the new Midland Pullman service. Recorded timings with two corridor bogies and track testing coach were just 3hrs 15mins outward and 3hrs 10mins return. Although primarily employed on traffic to the Fylde coast, the *Summer Jubilees* occasionally filled in on more mundane duties. An extract from a Lees (Oldham) MPD register reads: *Saturday 26th August 1961. No 45585 (26A) stopped on shed - left hand sander not working* - followed by a supplementary entry the following day: *Left hand piston bush blowing.*   **12TH AUGUST 1961 ● J. DAVENPORT**

No 45592 INDORE

Twenty one Jubilees, Nos (4)5574 - (4)5594 received names of locations within India which had links to the British Empire. Founded in 1715, ***Indore*** was a city in the central region of the country and locomotive No (4)5592 carried its name from 22nd January 1936 until withdrawal on 26th September 1964. It had always been a *Western Division* engine, working out of various depots, most latterly Carnforth from where it became a regular visitor until transferring to 9D in June 1964 for a final fling helping out with summer extras. No 45592 is near Euxton Junction with a Down excursion.   **12TH AUGUST 1964 ● J. DAVENPORT**

High in the Pennines, Diggle Junction is the rather remote setting for the 9.20am Leeds City to Manchester Exchange stopping train. A 'Crab' 2-6-0 drifts by past the signalbox on the Down main line whilst No **45710** *Irresistible* heads downgrade towards Greenfield. The lines in the right foreground form the Micklehurst loop, running down the left hand side of the Tame valley as far as Stalybridge where the tracks once again merge. **AUGUST 1959 ● J. DAVENPORT**

Reversing out of Glasgow Central and making its way to Polmadie MPD for servicing is No **45710** *Irresistible,* having arrived with an express from Manchester Victoria.

JUNE 1961 ● D. YOUNG COLLECTION

With the direct Kirkham to Blackpool Central line in the right foreground, Bradkirk signalbox stands between this line and that of the Kirkham to Poulton and Fleetwood on which Jubilee 4-6-0 No **45710** *Irresistible* makes haste with the 10.55am Manchester Victoria to Blackpool North/Fleetwood.

8TH SEPTEMBER 1962 ● P. FITTON

An unassisted train climbing Shap was always an impressive sight. One of Newton Heath's finest, according to many enginemen, was No **45710 *Irresistible*.** Despite having twelve bogies behind the tender, the crew are well in control of the morning Glasgow train - the loco had just returned from Crewe following a Light Intermediate! Although the first Jubilees arrived in 1935, it wasn't until 1943 that they regularly took over from the Patriots on these turns, by which time No 45710 was a 26A loco. It was withdrawn week ending 6th June 1964 and together with Nos 45578 *United Provinces* and 45737 *Atlas* (withdrawn the previous week), made their way to Gorton shed for storage where the front number and nameplates were removed. *Irresistible* ended up at Springs Branch in September, en route to Central Wagon Co. Ltd, Wigan for cutting up, whilst the other two were dealt with at C.P, Wood, Killamarsh, arriving there on 30th October 1964. **JULY 1958 ● J. DAVENPORT**

Once more on Glasgow express duty, caught taking water from Dillicar Troughs. At this time No **45710 *Irresistible*.** was still coupled to its original Fowler tender (ex No 6106) but would accompany three more of this type before becoming paired with Stanier No 10329 in February 1959 (ex 2-8-0 No 48601). **JULY 1952 ● D. YOUNG COLLECTION**

In the early 1960's it was customary, yet perhaps surprising, for Newton Heath to provide a Jubilee to work the 6.15am (Saturdays Only) Manchester Victoria to Bradford Exchange. The engine then returned to Lancashire later in the morning with a Mytholmroyd to Moston coal train. No **45710 *Irresistible*** rumbles off Todmorden Viaduct, working hard up the 1 in 182 and about to pass through the station with the working. The platform in the right foreground was used by trains going over Copy Pit and was known as the Burnley Bay.

AUGUST 1960 ● R.S. GREENWOOD

No 45664 NELSON

In order to bolster their depleted stock of Jubilees, Newton Heath took delivery of the four remaining examples at nearby Agecroft, deemed surplus to requirements there after a short period of storage. Nos 45590 *Travancore,* 45654 *Hood,* 45664 *Nelson* and 45716 *Swiftsure* arrived on 22nd June 1963, which helped offset the loss of a trio of old faithfuls during the previous winter. No 45700 *Amethyst* was surprisingly transferred to Derby whilst Nos 45701 *Conqueror* and 45702 *Colossus* were both withdrawn. This familiar location at west end of Manchester Victoria's No 12 platform finds No **45664 *Nelson*** eager to depart with a stopping train to Southport. These four engines were the last to receive 26A shedplates before re-coding took place the following September. In both *Travancore* and *Nelson's* cases this coincided with a further move to Warrington at the end of the Summer timetable. No 5664 had been a regular visitor at Manchester Victoria during the 1940's, being an almost permanent feature on the afternoon York (the 5.10pm) which was then a Sheffield Millhouses working.

12TH AUGUST 1963 ● J. CLARKE

Performing the same duty over two years later as No 45710 *Irresistible* (Page 82) is No **45623** *Palestine* passing Hall Royd Junction Signalbox, Todmorden. The loco, which arrived from Crewe South in March 1962 had a poor reputation amongst enginemen - perhaps borne out by the fact that it had previously been relegated to a depot whose duties were almost exclusively freight as early as December 1960.

13TH OCTOBER 1962 ● R.S. GREENWOOD

Once more engaged on freight duties, No **45623** *Palestine* is nicely illuminated creating an impressive exhaust at Denton Junction whilst working the 10.25am Adswood Sidings (Stockport) to Staley and Millbrook lightweight freight.

13TH DECEMBER 1962 ● G. COLTAS

The complexity of track and signalling ▷ in the environs of Preston Station are seen to good effect as No **45623** *Palestine* makes a spirited start into bright sunlight away from the platforms. The southbound train is one of empty parcels stock and is probably returning to the Manchester area.

26TH MARCH 1964 ● M. WELCH

The magnitude of holiday traffic on a summer Saturday often resulted in trains from the Manchester area using using little used routes to gain an approach to Preston. No **45623** *Palestine* having travelled via Tyldesley, treads cautiously through Hindley South and is about to take the spur to Amberswood East Junction, thus avoiding Wigan. The left fork over the rear of the train is the former Great Central line to Glazebrook which offered connections to the CLC and lines to the south of the city. **4TH AUGUST 1962** ● **E.F. BENTLEY**

No **45623** *Palestine* was a loco which in latter years rarely enjoyed the benefit of the cleaner's attention - a cursory wipe over the cab side number usually sufficed. The locomotive is working a fitted freight, the lamps signifying Class C - an express authorised to run at a maximum of 35mph which it will eventually achieve once having passed over Shap Summit. In the meantime Palestine toils up the gradient at little more than walking pace near Scout Green. It was taken out of service five weeks later, becoming the eighth Newton Heath Jubilee withdrawn from the shed. It then languished behind the station until mid 1965 when it was despatched to the private scrapyard of Central Wagon Co. Ltd, Wigan.

13TH JUNE 1964 ● **D. CASH**

No 45671 PRINCE RUPERT

On 24th March 1956, the Royal Train returned south after a visit to Aintree (for the Grand National) via the Midland line to Bedford where the Queen and Prince Philip would spend a few days at a nearby stately home. A pair of Jubilees, Nos 45580 *Burma* (24E) and 45671 *Prince Rupert* (26A - pilot engine) were the selected motive power. Newton Heath were well prepared for the occasion and the Jubilee spent several days in the 'Parlour' where it received a complete repaint, courtesy of Horwich Works providing their paint shop foreman and several painters. The shed kept their own set of specially polished buffers, drawbar hooks and screw couplings in the smithy for Royal Train locos. Needless to say, it remained pride of the shed until October 1957 when it moved to Longsight - much to the dismay of the staff. Shortly before this transfer, the immaculate No **45671 Prince Rupert** powers past Unity Brook near Kearsley with a Blackpool express.

27TH AUGUST 1957 ● N. FIELDS

The choice of motive power for a ramblers excursion from Manchester Victoria to Garsdale (C880) was flagship Jubilee No **45671 Prince Rupert.** It arrived at this remote outpost, near Ais Gill on the Settle & Carlisle line, 54 minutes late although the official reason for delay went unrecorded. On Friday, 28th June 1957 the engine found itself on Leeds (Holbeck) shed and was promptly borrowed to work the following morning's 9.55am Leeds City to Paignton, which acted as a relief to the 'Devonian'. No 45671 worked throughout to Bristol and did not return until 2nd July when it brought a Bristol to Newcastle train as far as Sheffield Midland, where it was relieved by V2 2-6-2 No 60942 of Heaton MPD. The Operating Department at Newton Heath were on the receiving end for once, being denied the use of one of their best Jubilees for a number of days.

14TH AUGUST 1955 ● J.M. BENTLEY

No 45705 SEAHORSE

The September 1963 reorganisation of motive power districts resulted in Newton Heath being re-coded 9D and placed under Longsight's jurisdiction. From this time until the end of steam, many locos found themselves re-allocated as a 'paper transfer' only and such was the case with No **45705 Seahorse** which moved over the city to Trafford Park in August 1964, having arrived at Newton Heath only two months earlier. This had always been a north of England locomotive seeing service at three depots only. It went new to Farnley Junction (23rd May 1935) then on to Blackpool (16th June 1956) before moving nominally to Newton Heath (June 1964). There is little doubt that this Jubilee would have been amongst the most common to regularly visit Manchester, firstly with the Newcastle or Hull to Liverpool Lime Street workings and then the commuter trains. Blackpool regarded this as one of their best and it frequently worked the London Euston expresses from the Lancashire coast. During the first week of its arrival, *Seahorse* is passing through Hatch End with a Down afternoon Inter Regional relief train.

27TH JUNE 1964 ● M.S. STOKES

The heavy influx of extra traffic on the West Coast Main Line throughout the summer timetable resulted in the 9.20am Manchester Victoria - Glasgow Central being routed via Hellifield and the S&C line to Carlisle. No **45705 *Seahorse*** brings the train off the ex L&Y and on to former Midland metals at Hellifield South Junction. This remote town had been an important railway outpost but by 1964 was a shadow of its former self. The engine shed, adjacent to the station, had closed the previous year as had the interchange sidings in view as evidenced by the recently lifted track. In much earlier days (1881), the L&Y opened a three road shed south east of the junction behind the approaching train, but this became an early casualty of the LMS, closing in 1927.   **4TH JULY 1964 ● AUTHOR'S COLLECTION**

Whilst at Trafford Park, the Jubilee was kept in immaculate condition by the shed staff who had a long association with the class. It regularly worked the 5.22pm Manchester Central to Buxton commuter train and became a high profile (in local circles) and much photographed loco as a result. It was entrusted to several railtours including this, the LCGB *High Peak Railtour* (1X82) where No **45705 *Seahorse*** relieved No 4472 *Flying Scotsman* at Cheadle Heath for the run to Birmingham. With an enthusiast craning for a better view from the leading window of Southern coaching stock, *Seahorse* rounds the Buxworth curve, attacking the rising gradient towards Chinley with the special. Although No 45705 received a 9E shedplate, official records show it remained at Newton Heath until withdrawal.

18TH SEPTEMBER 1965 ● M. WELCH

— No 45628 SOMALILAND —

Clutching his cherished notebook, a junior gricer is ideally placed to record engine numbers from an open carriage window. No **45628 *Somaliland*** gets away from Manchester Victoria with an eastbound train.

AUGUST 1961 ● **J.A. COX**

Still in grubby condition, the borrowed Jubilee heads an Up express through Lancaster. *(see page 78)*

AUGUST 1961 ● **D. CASH**

No 45716 SWIFTSURE

Having recently transferred from Agecroft MPD, No **45716** *Swiftsure* has few problems leaving Hindley North with a lightweight stopping train to Wigan, usually the province of a 2-6-4 tank engine. This Jubilee retained a Fowler tender and large cab side numerals until withdrawal in September 1964 - a consequence of spending 25 out of its 28 years in service at Carlisle Kingmoor and subsequent repairs at Glasgow St. Rollox.

13TH JULY 1963 ● **T. HEAVYSIDE**

Stubbins Junction, north of Bury, was the point at which the Bacup line diverged from that to Haslingden and Accrington. No **45635 *Tobago*** takes the latter, bypassing the station, with the 9.10am Bury Bolton Street to Skegness excursion (1X20) which the engine worked throughout *(see below).* Despite a badly leaking cylinder, the loco has a good head of steam for the assault on the five mile climb to Baxenden. The start of the 1963 Bury Wakes week would still involve a number of Newton Heath engines, but back in 1951 some 25,000 people deserted the town on 50 special trains during the traditional first week in July.　　**6TH JULY 1963 ● D. HAMPSON**

No 45635 TOBAGO

Driver Bob Hamilton casts a look back down his train prior to departure from Wigan (North Western) Station. In the early 1950's, No **45635 *Tobago*** together with Nos 45661 *Vernon* and 45671 *Prince Rupert* were most commonly used on the Glasgow trains because of their larger tenders. This engine made numerous visits to London over the years and was regularly used on supporters excursions to Wembley in May in conjunction with the FA and Rugby League Cup Finals. On 13th September 1951 *Tobago* found itself at Bedford St Johns, having been piloted by 0-6-0 No 43967 on the midday goods from Bletchley. This was usually a Willesden or Bletchley turn and was another case of 1A borrowing a visiting loco.

23RD DECEMBER 1958 ● A. HAYNES COLLECTION

Having been a most unusual visitor to Skegness the previous day, No **45635 *Tobago*** finds itself arriving further up the coast at Scarborough with a Sunday excursion train. The engine will certainly have returned to the Manchester area with a balancing working in the meantime.

7TH JULY 1963 ● J.A. PEDEN COLLECTION

A classic photograph of a Jubilee in action. The combination of a clean locomotive, coaching stock in the photogenic carmine and cream livery and that essential ingredient - a spot of sunshine, conspire to produce this most pleasing study. Passing through London's outer suburbs at Hatch End with a summer Saturday relief train for Manchester is No **45635** *Tobago.*   **13TH JULY 1957** ● **B.W.L. BROOKSBANK**

The 1 in 38 climb out of Accrington up Baxenden Bank presents few problems for a locomotive which regularly tackled Shap and Beattock in its prime. No **45635** *Tobago* has charge of the 5.10pm Nelson to Moston Class C Vans. The train, which travelled by way of Bury Bolton Street and the east fork through Knowsley Street, Castleton West and South Junctions, was often diagrammed for Jubilee haulage by this time.   **30TH MAY 1963** ● **E.F. BENTLEY**

No 45578 UNITED PROVINCES

Another Jubilee whose name had Indian connections was No 45578 *United Provinces*. This had been very much a Western Division locomotive until March 1962 when, like a few others about this period, retired to Newton Heath to work out its mileage. The 1.30pm Manchester Victoria to Carlisle remained a regular Jubilee working, although on Fridays only the service was extended to Glasgow and Edinburgh with the loco being exchanged at Carlisle on these occasions. No 45578 awaits departure from Platform 14 and will call at Bolton, Preston, Lancaster and Penrith - an overall journey time of exactly three hours. **11TH JULY 1963 ● G. COLTAS**

Just over one month later, the same loco was being utilised by Bank Hall MPD on a filling-in turn. The train is the lightweight 4.40pm from Liverpool Exchange returning to Blackpool Central, the rear portion having been detached at Preston bound for Skipton. No **45578 *United Provinces*** is approaching Ansdell Station and about to pass under the footbridge where the original station and a level crossing were once situated. On the right is Cambridge Road. **19TH AUGUST 1963 ● P. FITTON**

On 9th July 1739, Vernon was recalled to the Navy, promoted to 'Vice Admiral of the Blue' and ordered to command a force of six ships to the West Indies. Four months later Porto Bello in the Gulf of Mexico was captured and he returned a national hero. In line with the LMS policy of naming certain members of the Jubilee class with significant historical naval connections, No 5661 received the name *Vernon* on 4th February 1936. No **45661 Vernon** presents a glorious sight near Farington Junction with a Glasgow to Manchester express.

1959 ● J. DAVENPORT

A pair of Gresley wooden bodied artics followed by standard LMS non corridor stock complete the formation for a Sunday morning Manchester Victoria to Blackpool Central train. No **45661 Vernon** is at St. Annes and passing a L&Y lower quadrant signal still in situ.

18TH OCTOBER 1959 ● P. FITTON

The 10.50am Glasgow Central to Manchester Victoria train (via Kilmarnock) was the regular preserve of the Newton Heath Jubilees. The longer 236 mile journey using this route resulted in those members attached to the larger 4,000 gallon Stanier tenders monopolising the diagrams (Nos 45635/42/61/71), the smaller Fowler tenders' coal capacity being barely adequate. No **45661 *Vernon*** pauses at the immaculately maintained Dumfries Station with the service. The pair of prominent billboards beneath the gable end advertise local quality pork pies and sausages and William Younger's Tartan Bitter! **30TH AUGUST 1960 ● P. FITTON**

Arriving at Preston Station's No 6 platform with the 11.00am Windermere to Crewe is No **45661 *Vernon*** in ex-works condition. The Class A headlamps over the bufferbeam are correctly set, but that on the right hand running plate has sprung open - the result of an insecure clasp. Irrespective of the rain, the lamp will certainly be out - but will it be noticed by station staff or signalmen en route, or will it remain undetected until the locomotive reaches Crewe? The four-coach train combined here with a portion from Blackpool North. *Vernon* had earlier worked north with the 8.15am Preston - Windermere stopping train. **19TH JUNE 1964 ● P. FITTON**

Another Jubilee with a fine reputation was No 45712 *Victory* and despite being coupled to a Fowler 3,500 gallon tender, this loco was a regular performer on the Glasgow turns. The well groomed engine shows no signs of steam leakage and makes a fine sight near Tebay with the afternoon train (4.15pm departure from Manchester Victoria). It is reputed that this loco was used by Newton Heath during the 'Victory in Europe' celebrations in May 1945 to act as station pilot at Victoria - perhaps as a gesture of pride.

19TH APRIL 1954 ● I.S. PEARSALL

No 45712 VICTORY

Approaching Lostock Junction with an afternoon Blackpool/Fleetwood - Manchester Victoria express. The loco still appears steam tight but the standards of cleanliness have fallen, the cab side having received a wipe over from the footplate to properly reveal the number. **No 45712** *Victory* was a long standing Newton Heath engine, being based there from 17th October 1942 until 23rd February 1957 when, after a short period on loan, it left for Trafford Park then Kentish Town. On 14th February 1953, Bolton Wanderers played away at Luton Town and at least two excursions ran, hauled by Jubilees Nos 45712 *Victory* and 45710 *Irresistible*. Both engines then went to Kentish Town shed for servicing, but No 45712 failed and was replaced by No 45616 *Malta GC* (14B) for the return journey. It is noteworthy that *Victory* briefly returned with others as a seasonal transfer in the summer of 1961 *(see page 78)*. On14th September 1961, no fewer than three 26A Jubilees (Nos 45585 *Hyderabad*, 45679 *Armada* and 45712) were together on Rowsley shed, perhaps prompting that depot to borrow *Victory* as cover that evening to work one of their most prestigious trains, the 10.45pm from Rowsley to Somers Town Yard and return - a night out on its usual stamping ground. It was also observed working the 6.25am Darley Dale - Nottingham slow the previous week (7th September 1961).

JUNE 1956 ● J. DAVENPORT

A further trio of photographs featuring No 45654 Hood. The Jubilee is caught ascending Shap Wells at 11.47am whilst working a 'Locomotive Club of Great Britain' Manchester to Carlisle special. Rear end assistance is provided by Fairburn 2-6-2T No **42232**.

6TH NOVEMBER 1965 ● P. FITTON

After arrival at Manchester Victoria with the empty ▶ stock for an inter-regional excursion.

MAY 1966 ● J. CALDWELL

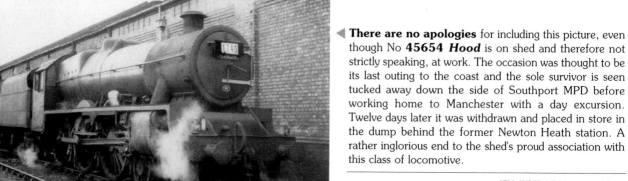

◀ **There are no apologies** for including this picture, even though No **45654 Hood** is on shed and therefore not strictly speaking, at work. The occasion was thought to be its last outing to the coast and the sole survivor is seen tucked away down the side of Southport MPD before working home to Manchester with a day excursion. Twelve days later it was withdrawn and placed in store in the dump behind the former Newton Heath station. A rather inglorious end to the shed's proud association with this class of locomotive.

4TH JUNE 1966 ● D. CASH

Safely negotiating the maze of points and signals to be found at the north end of Preston Station, Royal Scot Class 4-6-0 No **46140** *The King's Royal Rifle Corps* restarts the 4.55pm Manchester Victoria to Blackpool North past No 5 signal box. Passing in the opposite direction is Crewe South 8F 2-8-0 No **48502** with an Up Blue Circle cement train.   **26TH JUNE 1964** ● **P. FITTON**

THE ROYAL SCOT 4-6-0's

Approaching Preston from the south at Skew Bridge and once more on Blackpool duties is No **46139** *The Welch Regiment*. The two young gricers creeping down the embankment are caught side on to the engine and will be no doubt be admiring the nameplate after having 'clocked' the approaching front numberplate. When Newton Heath dispensed with their Britannia Pacifics to Neasden in September 1961 as a 'bad lot', they received Class 7 power in their place in the form of four Royal Scots (Nos 46133 *The Green Howards*, 46139 *The Welch Regiment*, 46140 *The King's Royal Rifle Corps* and 46142 *The York and Lancaster Regiment*) and one rebuilt Patriot (No 45522 *Prestatyn*), displaced from Kentish Town. Once again, they were intended for the Glasgow expresses but were also found wanting over the arduous route, although the Polmadie engines seemed to cope satisfactorily. The tried and trusted Jubilees returned for a final fling before dieselisation in 1962.   **1ST AUGUST 1962** ● **P. FITTON**

Rolling into Lancaster Castle Station with a combined Manchester/Liverpool to Glasgow train is the unique Royal Scot Class 4-6-0 No **46106 Gordon Highlander.** This particular locomotive still retained its parallel boiler at the close of the LMS period, after which it was renumbered in June 1948 and rebuilt three months later. The experimental fitting of square-shaped smoke deflectors in early BR days remained with the engine until withdrawal in December 1962.   **15TH OCTOBER 1960 ● P. FITTON**

In the early 1960s, the 2.50pm (Sundays Only) Manchester Victoria to Blackpool North was regularly booked for a Newton Heath Jubilee. A group of Manchester trainspotters regularly travelled on this train as far as Bolton, primarily in search of those ex-Horwich Works locos which could be found on Bolton shed. Notable examples were 0-6-0 No 44422 from Templecombe - deep in the heart of S&D territory and Bristol Barrow Road's 'Lanky' Pug 0-4-0ST No 51218, both of which happily survive in preservation. Occasionally Class 7 power would be provided and such was this case here. 4-6-0 No **46142 The York and Lancaster Regiment** moves out of the platform at Trinity Street Station en route to Chorley, Preston and the Fylde.

5TH AUGUST 1962 ● P. JORDAN

As the weather continues to close in over the environs of Leeds City Station, so three 'platform enders' make careful note of the arrival of No **46140 The King's Royal Rifle Corps** from the south with an inter-regional special - possibly bound for Scarborough. The dedicated Leeds gricers would have recorded this number many times before whilst working The Thames-Clyde express as a Kentish Town loco. Although the 'Scots' had been a common sight here throughout the 1950's, by the summer of 1961, Leeds Holbeck had dispensed with their remaining examples - transferred to Low Moor, leaving Jubilees to rule the roost. The two tank engines in evidence are probably on pilot duties.

JUNE 1962 ● AUTHOR'S COLLECTION

Royal Scot Class 4-6-0 No 46142 *The York and Lancaster Regiment* near St Annes with the 1.45pm Blackpool Central to Manchester Victoria train. The grounds of the 'Royal Lytham and St. Annes Golf Club' are visible to the right. This well known links course was founded in 1886 and officially opened by the Marquis of Lorne in 1898. The club hosted its first British Open tournament in 1926 at which time King George V gave his approval to add the word 'Royal' to it's title immediately before the event.

28TH APRIL 1962 ● P. FITTON

The 6.10pm Manchester Victoria to Southport express was a tightly timed prestige train and a regular working for the 'Scots' during their time at 26A. **No 46140 *The King's Royal Rifle Corps*** climbs away from the Salford suburbs on the Fast line towards Pendlebury, having stopped to pick up passengers only at Pendleton Broad Street. They rarely strayed off the Central Division but on January 13th and 14th, this loco and No 46133 *The Green Howards* were borrowed by Bristol Barrow Road MPD to cover an acute motive power shortage.

22ND APRIL 1963 ● E.F. BENTLEY

Passing over the water troughs, east of Lostock Junction with the 11.50 (SX) Blackpool Central to Manchester Victoria is No **46142 *The York and Lancaster Regiment*.** The building beside the Up slow line with a tank on its roof was the water treatment plant and pumping station, the supply being chemically treated with soda ash. **27TH MARCH 1963 ● E.F. BENTLEY**

A similar building existed alongside Brock Troughs which were situated eight miles north of Preston, immediately south of Garstang and Catterall Station. There had been a station here which closed on 1st May 1939 and was named after the Brockhole family, who were the local landowners. Two bridges in the vicinity carried their emblem, which were badger insignias and carved in stone. Replica badgers were set into artificial stone when rebuilt prior to electrification of the line which closely parallels the M6 motorway at this point. No **46140 *The King's Royal Rifle Corps*** approaches Garstang and Catterall Station with a northbound express. The first two coaches are an ex-LMS articulated 'twin'.

22ND JUNE 1963 ● R. FARRELL

No **46140 *The King's Royal Rifle Corps*** once again, but south of Preston at Euxton Junction with a lightweight train for Blackpool.

4TH JUNE 1963 ● G. COLTAS

THE IVATT CLASS 2-6-0's

The popular Ivatt Class 2 2-6-0's were ideally suited to Newton Heath's diverse range of duties and were regularly employed at Manchester Victoria on all manner of duties in and around the station. No **46484** stands on the spur adjacent to Turntable signalbox whilst acting as the Bays Pilot. A low sun on a fine evening results in dramatic shadow cast diagonally over the engine and running lines. The ramp end of Platform 11 which extended beyond Cheetham Hill Road bridge is prominent and trainspotters tended to congregate there - much to the consternation of officialdom. This particular locomotive had an unusual duty to perform on 17th June 1952. The 1.45pm Glasgow to Manchester Victoria was strengthened by 4 coaches on the rear for Stretford. The Ivatt 2-6-0, displaying Reporting Number C861, duly worked the train on via Miles Platting, Midland Junction, Ardwick Junction and the MSJ&A. It returned to Victoria 90 minutes later running in on the through westbound road before reversing on to the eastbound road, making use of the little-used trailing crossover. No 46484 then propelled the empty stock to Red Bank Carriage Sidings - a most unusual manoeuvre. **AUGUST 1959 ● K. FIELD**

As early as 6th June 1956, passenger services from Manchester Victoria to Bacup fell victim to the diesel era as one of the original routes selected by British Railways for Diesel Multiple Unit usage. The first sets had engines in only one coach and were occasionally 'found wanting' in adverse weather on the severe gradients. In the days of old, the Bacup branch had been very much L&Y 2-4-2T territory before latterly handing over to Stanier tanks working out of Bacup and Bury MPD's. Both Newton Heath and Bolton also had the odd turn. When Nos 46484-87 were delivered new to Newton Heath in November 1951, they were tried on the branch but the experiment didn't last long. Barely three months old, No **46485** stands at Bacup Station awaiting departure with a return train.

MARCH 1952 ● C.H.A. TOWNLEY

The Engineers' saloon has the company of an immaculate No **46485**, sauntering along on the Up West Coast Main Line north of Garstang.

28TH SEPTEMBER 1964 ● P. FITTON

Arriving in Platform 5 at Manchester Piccadilly Station is No **46452.** Note that locomotive exhaust has already made its mark on the refurbished passenger footbridge.

29TH APRIL 1964 ● T. NOBLE

Fifteen new engines (Nos 6405-19) were sent to the Central Division with Newton Heath receiving the last pair, Nos 6418/9. They were built as part of Lot 189 Crewe Order E465 and arrived in March 1947. Both were immediately employed on empty stock and pilot duties in and around Manchester Victoria. However in June 1948, they were sent to Darlington for trials over the Darlington - Kirkby Stephen - Penrith line as they were the only class of modern engine light enough to work on that road. They returned on 14th July after which date they were tried on the Divisional Engineers' train with great success. This had been the province of one of Newton Heath's best ex-L&Y 2-4-2 'radial' tanks throughout the LMS period. It was often the case in later years that the only loco on shed which bore a semblance of cleanliness was the Ivatt 2-6-0 kept respectable for this purpose, putting the rest of the gathering to shame! No **46418** makes haste coming off Smithy Bridge troughs and whilst a Permanent Way man appears to acknowledge the passing of his superiors in the saloon by standing to attention with spade in hand, his colleagues beyond seem oblivious to the event.

21ST SEPTEMBER 1962 ● I.G. HOLT

Lunchbreak at Hathersage for those civil engineers engaged on a bridge and tunnel inspection of Peak District lines. They have retired to the nearby 'Marquess of Granby Hotel' for refreshment, leaving Driver Stan (Slow Line) Jones and Fireman Richard Cort to idle away their time on the footplate. They were forbidden to leave their engine at this point - except in the case of emergency. Meanwhile, No **46485** basks in the Spring sunshine coupled to Saloon M45045M. When the party eventually returned off licensed premises, they brought two bottles of *Double Diamond* each for the crew in time honoured tradition.

23RD MAY 1967 ● M. WELCH

Unusually employed on the 9.05am Manchester Victoria to Wakefield Kirkgate stopping train is long standing resident No **46487**, awaiting departure from Castleton. This train was usually worked by a Normanton engine returning off the Up Normanton mail, but once again, on the occasion of an Easter Monday, the mail was cancelled. On the odd occasion when the mail was delayed and arrived too late for the engine to return, the bays pilot would be substituted, which usually proved to be a 'breadvan'. The train was then often curtailed at Todmorden as the following Leeds/Bradford express (the 9.28am from Victoria) had caught it up. No 46487 eventually bolstered the Lees (Oldham) allocation in September 1963 where it joined Nos 46484 and 46419 which had left Newton Heath during the previous year. When Lees depot closed in April 1964, a different trio arrived - Nos 46449/52/85. **18TH APRIL 1960 ● R.S. GREENWOOD**

One of the incumbents from Lees (Oldham) MPD, No 46452 is caught in the rather obscure surroundings of New Allen Street Junction, which is situated on the goods only branch midway between Miles Platting and the original *Manchester and Leeds Railway* terminus - Oldham Road Goods Station. It is engaged on the Philips Park Shunt, one of many such duties in the vicinity. This was previously performed by ex L&Y 3F 0-6-0 engines and involved working local trips between Moston, Brewery Sidings, Collyhurst Street, New Allen Street, Tank Yard, Oldham Road, Philips Park and Bradford Road Gas Sidings, as required. The line trailing in from the left is the spur connecting the goods station with Brewery Sidings, thus relieving the Miles Platting bottleneck of further congestion.

1965 ● J. CLARKE

Attending to parcels vans at Manchester Victoria is No 46490, a relatively late arrival at Newton Heath in August 1966 - but it was likely that the loco had performed similar pilot duties fifteen years earlier. New 2-6-0's from Darlington Works destined for the London Midland Region were delivered to Farnley Junction or Newton Heath depots for a couple of days 'running in' before proceeding to their own sheds. In No 46490's case this was on the Western Division at Bescot where it stayed, except for a five month spell at Saltley, before returning to the Central Division.

15TH APRIL 1967 ● G. COLTAS

Piloting an unidentified Class Five with a Rochdale to North Wales holiday train, No **46406** departs from New Hey leaving a fair residue of smoke in its wake. This was another late arrival - a victim of Bury's closure in April 1965 from where it had given stalwart service for many years and was a familiar sight in the locality. A lone mineral wagon and the condition of the track within the sidings suggests that the closure of goods facilities is imminent. **18TH JUNE 1966** ● **E.F. BENTLEY**

The following Saturday marked the start of the second week of the local holiday period and local cameraman Eric Bentley again ventured to New Hey to record a similar combination with a returning train from North Wales. It is the 9.50am Llandudno to Manchester Victoria, extended to Oldham Mumps via Rochdale and another ex Bury engine, No **46412** is in evidence, piloting Trafford Park Class Five No **45352** into the platform - arrival time 1.17pm. **25TH JUNE 1966** ● **E.F. BENTLEY**

Ivatt 2-6-0 No 46418 was a rare breed. In common with Jubilee 4-6-0 No 45701 *Conqueror*, the locomotive spent its entire life working out of Newton Heath until its withdrawal in January 1967. It obviously worked round the Oldham Loop over the years on many trains and, one suspects, partnered shedmate No **45702 *Colossus*** on more than one occasion. The pair are at Jubilee Crossing on the approach to New Hey with an excursion from Oldham Werneth bound for Barrow-in- Furness. An ex-LMS articulated set leads the formation.

23RD APRIL 1962 ● R.S. GREENWOOD

It was unusual to see an Ivatt 2-6-0 on local passenger work on the Oldham Loop. The suburban services between Manchester Victoria, Oldham and Rochdale during the BR period were monopolised by an army of Class 4 2-6-4 tanks of the Fairburn, Stanier and Standard variety before handing over to Diesel Multiple Units. No **46437** is nearing Heyside during the final week of steam operation.

4TH JULY 1958 ● P. HUTCHINSON

The Ivatt 2-6-0s were originally considered as possible replacements for the aged ex-L&Y 'A' Class 0-6-0s, but thirteen years later the veterans were still in evidence - a testament to their longevity. Both classes are seen here, working alongside each other on 'Wallside Pilot' duties with Nos **46411** and **52431** awaiting their next duties. They are caught from an open carriage window which is part of a Southport train standing in Platform 11. There is evidence of the fire being thrown out on more than one occasion and, being situated opposite Number 12 Platform, near to the buffet, hardly created an ideal atmosphere for the multitude of passengers awaiting departure from here. The 'A' Class finally departed the scene in May 1961.

MARCH 1960 ● J.A. COX

By the summer of 1966, Newton Heath still had twelve members to call on, including three of the final batch of 25 built at Swindon for the Western Region in 1952/3. They were later outshopped in unlined green, very much in keeping with GWR tradition. No **46505** arrived in August from an unlikely source - Saltley. It had previously spent the greater part of its life as an Oswestry engine working over the Cambrian Section. Despite being encrusted with grime, giving no clue as to its true livery, this was the best of the trio (the others were Nos 46504/06 which had arrived via Bolton). By June 1967 the depot had cleared their stocks of the class. No 46505 went to Buxton for a further month's service, whilst the remaining seven locos were withdrawn. The loco is seen passing light engine through Rochdale Station on the Down Goods Loop'.

OCTOBER 1966 ● BERNARD CRICK

The footbridge at Newton Heath Station offered panoramic views of the shed yard (east end) extending to St Mary's Road turntable (out of camera to the left), the junction and signalbox where the main line diverges for Miles Platting and the newer Manchester Loop line direct to Manchester Victoria. Lastly the broad expanse of Lightbowne Carriage Sidings which can be seen through the exhaust of Ivatt No **46437**. The loco is engaged on one of the numerous trip workings to nearby Moston Exchange Sidings, having approached from the Miles Platting direction. Its cleanliness suggests it as being the loco recently used on the engineers' special workings.

JUNE 1961 ● AUTHOR'S COLLECTION

In LMS and early BR days, the Beswick Shunt Engine was the province of Belle Vue MPD. Upon that shed's closure in March 1956, the duty was transferred to Newton Heath who provided Jinties and ex L&Y 2F 0-6-0 saddle tanks. Approaching Bradford Road Gasworks is one of the earlier Midland variety, No **47202** equipped with condensing apparatus, returning from Beswick to Brewery Sidings with empty bolster wagons, having completed its stint on Pilot duty. The impending closure of Agecroft MPD brought about its arrival in August 1966 but it was withdrawn four months later. *(see overleaf)* **SEPTEMBER 1966 ● M. CORT**

THE FOWLER 0-6-0 'JINTY' TANKS

Another member that had a short innings at Newton Heath was No **47362.** Fireman Albert Dean is on the footplate and again the turn is the Beswick Pilot. By this time Diesel Shunters were being used on this and other local duties, but after a couple of 'runaways', most old hands still preferred to take a steam loco off shed. **23RD OCTOBER 1965 ● M. CORT**

Busy shunting vans under Rhodes Bank footbridge, Oldham is Jinty 0-6-0
No **47383**. Thanks to the efforts of Frank Cronin, Bernard Crick and others,
the loco survives in preservation at the Severn Valley Railway, Bridgnorth.
Newton Heath took over Lees (Oldham) MPD's duties, of which this was one,
upon closure on 13th April 1964.   **29TH APRIL 1966 ● R.S. GREENWOOD**

About to position yet another set of loaded minerals on the coal stage
road is veteran 0-6-0T No **47202**. The yard shunter, standing on the bottom
step with pole in left hand, hangs on with the right for the short trip alongside
the shed building.   **SEPTEMBER 1966 ● P. JORDAN**

Another ex-Midland 3F, No 47207 brings a pair of
tar wagons off the Royton Branch whilst engaged on pilot
duty. The view is from the top of steps off Holyrood
Street bridge looking down to a footpath between the
tracks leading to Royton Junction Station.

18TH FEBRUARY 1961 ● D. CASH

◄ **A train of coal destined for Higginshaw Gas Works**
awaits the signal to ascend the incline.

19TH OCTOBER 1966 ● R.S. GREENWOOD

The Saturday morning Royton Pilots, 'A' Class No
52341 and Jinty No 47547 returned to Newton
Heath shed via Rochdale and Castleton on this particular
day due to the weight of holiday traffic in the Oldham
area. The crew on the Jinties footplate check for clear
signals as the pair approach Rochdale East Junction,
descending from the Milnrow Road bridge. Meanwhile,
the storm sheet is being attended to on the footplate of
the ex L&Y loco.

18TH JUNE 1960 ● R.S. GREENWOOD

Thrusting the Jinties into the limelight. The 'Manchester Rail Travel Society' organised a 'Three Counties Railtour' involving two of the three engines remaining in service at Newton Heath. (No 47388 was the other). No **47202**, one of the early Johnson 3F's fitted with condensing apparatus, was pilot engine and No **47383** (eventually preserved at No 47202's expense) train engine. The pair relieved Stanier 2-6-4 Tank No 42644 at Bury Bolton Street for the onward journey via Clifton Junction to Manchester Victoria. Then, not to be outdone, the Jinties got the better of a local DMU on the climb up Miles Platting bank, much to the delight of the enthusiasts on board. After travelling via Droylsden and Denton Junctions, the 0-6-0T's were, in turn, relieved by Ivatt 2-6-2T No 41204 at Stockport Edgeley for the onward journey to Buxton. It was later reported that No 47202 was working with only one manual injector! Birds are caught in mid flight as the train crosses the murky waters of the River Irwell en route from Bury to Manchester. Outwood Viaduct, a magnificent Grade 2 listed structure which was built in 1881 by Andrew Handyside of Derby, has a pipeline passing through the brick arches at low level.

26TH NOVEMBER 1966 ● E.F. BENTLEY

After the demise of the former L&Y classes, Jinties were often employed at the shed on the coal shunt. No **47388** is busy collecting and receiving wagons which were stabled immediately behind Newton Heath's Up platform. Visible over the east yard and beyond the diesel maintenance depot and 'Parlour' is the austere enginemens' lodging house, then empty and only a shell. Various Operating Departments had made use of the 66-bed 'barracks' from 1890 until its closure in 1964. The building was demolished in 1967.

SEPTEMBER 1966 ● P. JORDAN

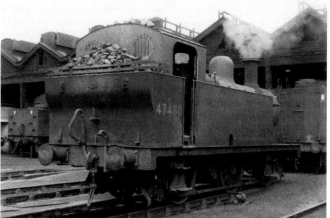

Another member working at its home depot was No 47480 acting as the Shed Pilot. Closer examination of this picture reveals an interesting past. It clearly shows the apparatus fitted for use on the one time push-pull service between Swansea St. Thomas and Brynamman. This loco (and others) worked out of Swansea Paxton Street, Upper Bank and its sub shed at Gurnos until March 1957 when it headed north to Walton MPD. This wasn't the only engine with Western connections however. In December 1956, Nos 47301/3/5 and 47425 arrived from Bromsgrove for a short period, displaced as Lickey bankers by the newer Hawksworth Pannier Tanks, Nos 8400 - 8406 which had a slightly higher tractive effort.

OCTOBER 1965 ● G. HARROP

A most unlikely combination taking the Miles Platting line by Newton Heath Junction Signalbox are Stanier Class Five No **45083** and Jinty 0-6-0 No **47383** which is travelling out of steam as part of the train. The locomotive had been at 9D for just over a year but had been earmarked for further work at Williamthorpe Colliery and was photographed in the process of transfer to Westhouses MPD within a Moston Sidings to Gowhole freight.

FEBRUARY 1967 ● M. CORT

THE STANIER CLASS 8F 2-8-0's

Designed by Stanier during 1935, the heavy duty 8Fs proved so successful that they were generally regarded as the engines that 'won the war' - although in fairness, the Stanier Class Fives and LNER V2s also shared similar acclaim. After hostilities ended, the 1945 allocation lists reveal that LMS locos (others also worked on the GW and LNE lines) were based exclusively at Midland and Western Division depots with a small number in Scotland. By 1950 however, no fewer than 150 engines had infiltrated the Central Division with large numbers arriving at Newton Heath. This influx soon rendered the L&Y 0-8-0's extinct and the 'Austin Sevens' became the secondary freight locomotive but they were soon to be on the move again *(see overleaf)*. One of the new arrivals, No **48705** is near Handforth with a Crewe bound freight. Sister engine, No 48707 which arrived at the same time, reached Edinburgh over the 1949 Christmas period in ex-works condition. It had arrived on Tyneside after being borrowed by Leeds or York and as the Heaton turntable was out of commission, it went further north.

28TH MARCH 1949 ● T. LEWIS

After 1963, the old Central Division and Western Division north of Crewe were encompassed as the North Western Lines and coinciding with this reorganisation, 8Fs from the Midland Division were becoming surplus and the migration north began. By 1965, over 200 were at work in the area with 14 based at Newton Heath. 2-8-0 No **48106** makes a fine sight leaving Rochdale with a morning train of eastbound coal empties. It was a long standing Birkenhead engine which arrived via Warrington in November 1963 and the miniature snow plough may well have been the one fitted to WD No 90338 which was withdrawn from the shed during the same month.

6TH MARCH 1964 ● E.F. BENTLEY

Those trainspotters occupying the bank opposite Skew Bridge signalbox may well have been disappointed at the sight of an 8F clanking up the main line on an express passenger train rather than an unusual Jubilee. The Operating Department however had no such reservations regarding deployment of those engines which were fitted with improved wheel balancing. One such loco, No **48148** has just crossed the River Ribble and leaves Preston in its wake whilst in charge of excursion No C399 which comprises a smart set of 10 carriages of which nos 4 and 5 are roofboarded.

1960 ● D. YOUNG COLLECTION

No sooner had the Central Division received a number of 8Fs, the London Midland Region of British Railways began to accept WD 2-8-0s which had remained in store since the end of the war. A motive power reshuffle resulted in the 8Fs moving away to the Western and Midland Divisions (between October 1950 and August 1951) whilst the WD's took their place. Seven years later, the next five 8F's to arrive included this one, No **48553** in October 1958. It is descending Miles Platting bank on the approaches to Manchester Victoria Station with a transfer freight for Ordsall Lane. Four of these engines (including No 48553) moved on to Patricroft in December 1963 to help ease a crisis brought about by the withdrawal of their 'Super D' 0-8-0s.

6TH APRIL 1960 ● G. COLTAS

The onset of dieselisation at Staveley (Barrow Hill) in the Spring of 1964 resulted in a handful of 8F's being added to Newton Heath's allocation. One of these, No **48533** toils upgrade on the CLC towards Bredbury Junction with empty minerals. Sighting restrictions beyond Brinnington tunnel resulted in this pair of imposing lattice lower quadrant signals being situated immediately east of Ashton Road bridge on the Down side of the line. The splitting home is off for Woodley Junction whilst that on the left directed traffic towards Romiley Junction.

3RD MARCH 1966 ● G. COLTAS

Driver Johnny O'Gara and Fireman George Bingham ended the year with a bump. On 28th December 1966 they were in charge of 8F No **48758** and whilst drifting downgrade into Moston Exchange Sidings with empty minerals, Johnny braked but with nil effect. The load pushed them on and as George hastily screwed the handbrake hard on, Johnny applied full brake and wound the 8F into full reverse gear and started pumping the regulator. It slowed the 8F down but ahead, a Standard 4-6-0 from Bolton, No 73014 stood fouling their path whilst the crew were having their 'snaps' in the shunters cabin. The almost broadside collision bent part of the Standard's motion behind the right hand cylinder after which it was on shed under light repair for a few days. The following year, a similar working records No 48758 leaving the Down Sidings at Royton Junction with a Mumps to Moston freight. **6TH JUNE 1967 ● P. HUTCHINSON**

Garstang and Catterall Station is the setting for 8F No **48318** hurrying through towards Preston with an Up mixed freight. The rather clean building in the centre background is the local creamery which had rail access. *The Garstang and Knott End Railway* made use of the outer face of the Down platform and paralleled the main line for a distance before deviating west. The facilities here outlived steam, closing on 3rd February 1969 with the station building being demolished two years later. Alas the creamery is also but a memory. **13TH AUGUST 1965 ● P. FITTON**

The magnitude of mineral traffic from the Yorkshire coalfield over the Pennines regularly resulted in an imbalance of brake vans left in various Lancashire sidings. Loaded trains consisted of up to 45 wagons, whereas the returning empties could number as many as 60. The strays would then be grouped to form part of a returning rake. One such combination sees No **48557** passing Castleton East Junction signalbox bound for Healey Mills.

1965 ● J. CLARKE

Stanier 2-8-0 No **48612** ambles through the middle road at ▶ Bolton Trinity Street Station with returning newspaper vans from Heysham to Red Bank. This was normally a Class Five duty but nicely illustrates the versatility of these locos.

2ND SEPTEMBER 1967 ● P. HUTCHINSON

Threading its way past Miles Platting Junction Signalbox and about to take the Ashton Branch towards Philips Park is No **48090**. The freight has been banked tender first up the incline by an unidentified Class Five which is about to drop off and return to the Wallside.

AUGUST 1967 ● R. CORT
▼

Permanent Way Men 'In Possession'. A light covering of snow greeted the crew of 8F No **48321** on this cold December morning in 1967. They are working wrong line through Newton Heath station, propelling 2 bogie flats with brake van at either end attending to a section of line adjacent to St Mary's Road bridge, some 100 yards distant.   **10TH DECEMBER 1967 ● R. CORT**

Kirkham North Junction, the scene of incessant activity during the summer months as traffic passed through heading to and from the Fylde coast. 8Fs were a common sight on excursion trains, especially the few with a star beneath the cab side number. This signified a counterbalancing of the moving parts, permitting faster speeds, thus enabling suitability for passenger work. No **48318** was one such engine and is heading down the direct Marton line with a Todmorden - Blackpool Central train (1T52). These excursions ran either via Copy Pit or Bolton, largely depending on where the loco and stock originated from. In this case it is probably the former, being a Newton Heath engine with coaches from Lightbowne Sidings. The loco would be ideally suited for the arduous climb in the early stages of the journey.   **11TH JULY 1964 ● P. FITTON**

A barren wasteland represents the grim surroundings on the approaches to that former Midland Railway stronghold, Ancoats Goods Station. By 1968 what traffic remained was mostly in the hands of Newton Heath Class Fives or 8Fs. One of the last arrivals was No **48529** after the closure of Edge Hill during May and local cameraman Dave Jessop ventured down Great Ancoats Street to capture it at work. It was withdrawn upon the closure of the shed to steam on 1st July along with ten other 8Fs.　　　　　**JUNE 1968** ● **D. JESSOP**

◀ **Making good progress whilst passing Mirfield MPD** with express freight is No **48046.** The ex L&Y depot was into its final year of operation and prominent behind the engine is the 'coal hole' which remained in use until the end. Although the LMS failed to invest in upgrading the coaling facilities, they did install colour light signalling as early as July 1932 in the immediate vicinity. A pair are visible over the train and what appears to be an English Electric Type 4 heading northbound. This particular 8F was noteworthy, being one of 51 members requisitioned by the War Department from existing stock in October 1941. It was converted to oil burning and despatched to Iran as WD No 599, eventually returning in 1949.

28TH JULY 1966 ● **AUTHOR'S COLLECTION**

The late afternoon Hollinwood to Moston transfer freight was usually worked tender first. No **48745** is seen on the embankment, west of Castleton Sidings with the train. This loco was an unlikely arrival from Longsight in November 1958 - a shed not normally associated with 8F's.

28TH APRIL 1960 ● **R.S. GREENWOOD**

THE FOWLER CLASS 7F 0-8-0's

The 7F 0-8-0's designed by Sir Henry Fowler were comparatively short-lived. Of a class which originally numbered 175, only half remained in service in 1950 - barely 20 years after introduction. Although powerful and economical on coal and water, they were prone to running hot and as a consequence were restricted to working over shorter distances and never quite reached expectations. As well as plying their trade up and down the Calder Valley, they were regularly seen at Gowhole with transfer freights from North Manchester but rarely ventured beyond to Rowsley with other turns. Popularly referred to in later years as 'Austin Sevens', the locomen's original nickname was 'Baby Austins', a topical name echoing the road vehicles of the day. No **49515** works a lengthy train in the Hebden Bridge area.

1958 ● **J.A. COX**

The early days of Nationalisation was very much a transitionary period for freight motive power in the area as Stanier 8Fs were arriving in quantity, soon to be replaced by WD 2-8-0s. Meanwhile the 'Austin Seven' 0-8-0s kept soldiering on. Numbers were initially augmented by those transferred off the Midland Division (where they proved unpopular), thus concentrating what remained on the Central Division. Newton Heath had 23 as of 1st January 1948 but the situation remained fluid and continuing withdrawals brought that total down to 8 by 1957. Prior to entering works for overhaul and renumbering, No **9565** is hard at work forging down the Calder Valley near Sowerby Bridge with a coal train.

MAY 1948 ● **G. SHARPE**

Drifting downgrade with loaded minerals towards Brinnington tunnel and Stockport Tiviot Dale is 0-8-0 No **49624**. The train is passing the rather remote but nevertheless busy Bredbury Junction Signalbox. The class were uncommon visitors to the CLC and were more likely to be seen crossing the short viaduct in the distance with transfer freights to Gowhole. This carries the former Great Central and Midland Joint line between Romiley Junction and Ashburys Junction.

c1958 ● W.A. BROWN

Having passed through Middleton Junction, a lengthy mixed goods train is approaching Vitriol Works Signalbox and the Chadderton Power Station complex behind 0-8-0 No **49508**, making sedate progress and probably bound for Moston Exchange Sidings. The fireman is taking a breather and with a decking pipe hanging over the cab side, it suggests that the footplate may well have just been washed down.

1959 ● J. DAVENPORT

About to pass through the platforms at Preston Station is the same locomotive, No **49508**. This was destined to become the last survivor of the class and one of the few which was outshopped at Horwich in BR days. After a period at Bury, it became a 26A engine in March 1953 and eventually moved to Agecroft in November 1960 for a final year in service. The class had originally numbered 175 and were the last conventional inside cylindered 0-8-0's to be designed. Five were converted to oil burning in 1947 (Nos 9511/33/613/42/ 70), but only No 9511 survived to be reconverted to coal. Three of these, including No 9511 were Newton Heath engines at the time.

c1952 ● E. WOODS

A deserted Rochdale Station is about to witness the rousing echoes of Fowler Class 7F No **49624** passing through on its way north with the 12.50pm Middleton Junction to Healey Mills coal empties. Suburban traffic was intensive here and a feature were the 2,000 gallon parachute water columns serving all four departure platforms. The one in full view is designated '215 - Bury' whilst '214 - Manchester' is partially visible. Nos '212 - Facit' and '213 Oldham' were situated at the opposite end. They dated from L&Y days and additional columns could be found by the East Junction signalbox, serving the Down Goods Loop and the turntable road whilst a standard column sufficed for the Up Goods Loop.   **28TH MAY 1960** ● **R.S. GREENWOOD**

An unusual sight trundling through Hebden Bridge Station was a clean loco engaged on freight work and this westbound train of coal is probably destined for Moston Exchange Sidings. The bright red buffer beam betrays the fact that Fowler Class 7F No **49565** is undoubtedly ex-Horwich Works, having received its new BR number in the process. Unfortunately it soon became the first Standard 0-8-0 to be withdrawn from service and cutting up began the following year on 10th April 1949, again at Horwich.

1948 ● **KIDDERMINSTER RAILWAY MUSEUM**

The rugged lines of Fowler Class 7F No 49661 seem somehow in keeping with the dull overcast conditions as it toils through Cheadle (CLC) with mixed freight. The class were steam braked only and therefore incapable of working fitted freights or passenger services, but the final 15 locos (Nos 9660 - 9674) were coupled to riveted Fowler tenders fitted with coal rails to help protect the 4 ton capacity. Despite their reputation, some of the older hands on the Central Division considered them superior to Stanier 8Fs when faced with a standing start on an incline with a heavy train.

c1953 ● G. COLTAS

The goods and coal yards at Royton are overflowing to capacity in this view looking towards the station. The morning Royton Shunt Engine has arrived with the 10.45am from the nearby Junction after which nearly two hours are allotted for shunting duties. 'Austin Seven' No **49508** will then work the 12.45pm Royton to Hartford Sidings (Oldham). With so much goods traffic in evidence and a healthy patronage of passenger services at the time, it is hard to believe that three years later the rail amenity was under the threat of closure.

1958 ● B. HILTON

In the early 1950's, wooden bodied wagons were the order of the day for moving coal around the country. They were less than uniform and this motley assortment still includes examples in private ownership. 0-8-0 No **49560** trundles along at their head on Class 'F' empties passing alongside Mirfield shed. The original northlight roof was retained over the offices and stores (in view) whilst the engine shed itself was converted to single pitch style as part of the 1935 LMS modernisation plan.

c1950 ● B.W.L. BROOKSBANK

The rather forlorn surroundings of Smithy Bridge Down platform greet an equally forlorn 'Austin Seven' No **49508** working a lengthy train of empty mineral wagons. **10TH APRIL 1960** ● **R.S. GREENWOOD**

The only time of the week when Permanent Way men could take possession of busy stretches of line during daylight were Sundays - track maintenance and relaying duties being the primary activities. 'Austin Seven' No **49618** stands 'Bang Road' at Castleton Station whiling away the time whilst a dozen or so men are busy at work. Although the enginemen might be earning time and three quarters, long periods of inactivity made for a boring shift. **6TH MARCH 1960** ● **R.S. GREENWOOD**

Approaching Ramsbottom with the afternoon 4.45pm Bacup to Moston is 0-8-0 No **49666**, a regular Newton Heath 7F working. These were the largest freight engines permitted over the northern part of the route, thus barring the Stanier and WD 2-8-0s. The train was often heavily loaded, having picked up traffic at various stations en route, much of which came from the Waterfoot slipper manufacturers. An occasional feature was an intermediate brake van half way down the train manned by a railway policeman as a precaution against pilferage. It offered a connection at Moston to immediately forward wagons on the overnight fitted express goods to Camden. After withdrawal of the 7F's, Class 4F 0-6-0s Nos 44022, 44311 and 44543 took over, by which time loadings were significantly reduced.

20TH MAY 1955 ● B. ROBERTS

THE CLASS 2P 2-4-2 TANKS

Large numbers of Aspinall's 2-4-2 tank engines were prominent at Newton Heath throughout the L&Y and early LMS periods handling the intensive suburban services, but the arrival of the Stanier and Fairburn 2-6-4T's quickly brought about their demise. By January 1948, a mere 7 remained on the books - the last to go being No 50859 - withdrawn in November 1953. No **50746** is caught working an Engineers' Special at Lees, Oldham before its transfer away to Blackpool and finally Southport, where it took up residence as the Chapel Street Station Pilot until withdrawal in February 1961.

1948 ● J. DAVENPORT

THE 'PUG' CLASS 0F 0-6-0 SADDLE TANKS

Stabled in the West yard are two of the diminutive ex-L&Y 0-4-0ST 'Pugs', Nos **11234** and **11207**. Unfortunately pictures of this class of locomotive at work during any period *(other than Irwell Street Goods)* appear to be almost non-existent, so I make no apologies for including this view showing both engines in steam. By 1948 the shed had been reduced to a pair, No 11234 and 11222. The former was the last of the 'potato engines' working regularly at Oldham Road Goods Depot until its transfer to Bank Hall in February 1950 at which time it was renumbered. No 11222, renumbered in August 1949, was the spare engine and moved away to Goole at the same time. At the Grouping, Newton Heath had nine on allocation, a total which was maintained throughout the greater part of the LMS period.

1935 ● **W.R.P. LEES**

THE CLASS 2F 0-6-0 SADDLE TANKS

During the summer months of June and July in the 1950's, it was possible to obtain pictures of ex-L&Y 2F 0-6-0STs out on the main line in daylight, working the 8.35pm Royton Junction to Brewery Sidings goods. The train also enabled the engine to return to its home depot after a day's work in the area *(see overleaf)*. No **51497** was a regular performer and local cameraman Brian Hilton photographed the train on consecutive evenings from the bridges immediately west of Royton Junction Station. *Left:* Woodstock Occupation Bridge is the vantage point for the shorter of the two trains whilst Bullcote Lane Bridge *(right)* offered this view looking back towards Royton with the Woodstock Spinning Mill on the horizon. **12TH/13TH JUNE 1958** ● **B. HILTON**

The Royton Junction Shunt involved visits to Higginshaw Gas Works, which were within close proximity of the station and approached via a steep incline off the Royton Branch. No **51458** and brake van descend the bank, having delivered coal and coke by working wrong line to gain access to the private sidings. Another interesting part of the loco's duty was the early morning sanding of the rails between Middleton Junction and Oldham Werneth *(the Werneth incline)*.

1958 ● B. HILTON

NEWTON HEATH TRIP ENGINES - No. 35. CLASS 2F TANK (L&Y 0-6-0)

	MO arr. am.	dep. am.		SO arr. am.	dep. am.
Newton Heath Shed	-	5.40LE, A.	Newton Heath Shed	-	5.22LE, A.
Royton Jn.	5.55	-	Werneth	5.33	B
		Shunt			Shunt
Royton Jn	-	6.40	Werneth	-	8.57
Royton	6.55	7.20LE	Royton	9.10	9.40
Werneth	7.30	B	Werneth	9.51	-
		Shunt		**arr. pm.**	**arr. pm.**
Werneth	-	8.57	Werneth	-	1.35
Royton Jn.	9.10	9.40	Royton Jn.	1.47	2.15EBV
Werneth	9.51	-	Royton	2.20	-
	MSX				Shunt
Newton Heath Shed	-	5.22A.	Royton	-	3.20
Royton Jn.	5.33	-	Royton Jn.	3.30	4. 0
		Shunt	Werneth	4.12	-
	SX arr. pm.	**dep. pm.**			Shunt
Werneth	-	12.33LE	Werneth	-	5.30LE
Newton Heath Shed	12.48	2. 3LE	Newton Heath Shed	5.42	-
Royton Jn.	2.21	C			
		Shunt			
Royton Jn.	-	9.30LE			
Newton Heath Shed	9.50	-			

A - Sands rails between Middleton Jn. & Werneth
B - Tests vacuum fitted vehicles
C - Works trips to Higginshaw & Royton Jn. as required

The Civil Engineering Shops at Newton Heath, formerly part of the old Carriage and Wagon Works finds No **51415** on duty. A pair of 'Pugs' worked here during the L&Y and early LMS periods.

1957 ● M.S. WELCH

The 3.50pm Bolton East Junction to Bullfield Sidings transfer freight (Reporting No BN75) had always been an interesting train as it was usually powered by old and small engines or locos ex-Horwich Works running in from Bolton Shed. It went bunker first and had to work to time to avoid main line trains at the Junction. On this occasion, Newton Heath's remaining 0-6-0ST No **51371** was on duty, working on loan at Bolton. This once numerous class were rebuilds of the original L&Y F15's designed by W. Barton Wright and introduced in August 1876 (coinciding with the opening of Newton Heath MPD). Although the twenty survivors in 1960 were scattered over the old L&Y system, three were in use as works shunters at Crewe and another four, which retained their LMS numbers, were service locos at Horwich Works. No 11305 of the latter was the last to be withdrawn, in December 1964.

27TH JULY 1960 ● D. HAMPSON

A class of engine strongly associated with the shed were the L&Y 'A' 0-6-0s. No fewer than 56 members carried 26A shedplates at one time or another during the BR period - a total no doubt supplemented by even more in earlier days. This striking picture of No **52275** piloting Patricroft Standard Class Five No **73074** is significant. W633 is a returning holiday special from Llandudno to Oldham and despite the steady climb from Shaw and Royton Junction, the footplate crews appear to be able to communicate! During April 1958 the 0-6-0 was officially transferred to Horwich, possibly covering for a works shunter, before returning one month later - the only engine to experience such a move in BR days.
23RD AUGUST 1958 ● **B. HILTON**

THE EX-L&Y 'A' CLASS 0-6-0's

One of the many that gravitated to the shed was No **52230**. It was one of a trio (Nos 52119 and 52269 were the others) which were previously based at an unlikely outpost - Bangor MPD - former LNWR territory. It arrived via Springs Branch (Wigan) during May 1958. The decrepit condition of the smokebox door is slightly relieved by a recently affixed shedplate. No 52230 is caught trundling past the shed building busily engaged on the coal shunt - a continuous operation with a relieving engine taking over as required. Closer inspection reveals the spectacle plate swivelled half open whilst the storm sheet appears to be hanging down from the cab roof. That most essential item on the footplate - a billy can, is also visible. Why the loco is showing Class A headlamps is a mystery.

AUGUST 1958 ● **J. DAVENPORT**

In 1948, **Newton Heath** had to provide anything up to 16 L&Y Class 3Fs on weekdays to satisfy the various trip, shunt and pilot workings associated with the shed. 24 locos were on allocation at the time. One such duty was the Hollinwood Shunt Engine whose details are outlined below. Gently simmering away in the goods yard is No **12518,** one of a second batch built at Horwich in 1909 with superheated round top firebox boilers and later converted to round top saturated. This loco was an early casualty, being withdrawn in February 1949 without ever receiving its BR number.

11TH MAY 1948 ● G. SHUTTLEWORTH

HOLLINWOOD SHUNT ENGINE
No 1 NEWTON HEATH CLASS 3F (L&Y 0-6-0)

6.42am to 8.25pm SX   6.42am to 2.25pm SO

After banking 6.25am Brewery Sidings - Hollinwood from Dean Lane MO.

Shunt and test vacuum fitted vehicles daily.

Works 2.25pm Hollinwood - Ashton Moss SO.

A Lanky 'A' Class was also provided for Trip No 36 which involved a daily outing to New Hey. L&Y 0-6-0 No **52270** reverses five minerals and a flat wagon on to the Down main line and under Two Bridges Road before setting back into the goods yard. This rear view nicely illustrates the loco crew concentrating on the job in hand. The fireman has acknowledged the shunters 'right away' call and conveyed the message to his driver whose view is impeded. They will then couple up to another five wagons and brake van visible in front of the Up side station building before departure.

28TH MAY 1960 ● R.S. GREENWOOD

NEWTON HEATH TRIP ENGINE - No. 36. CLASS 3F (L&Y 0-6-0)

	arr. am.	dep. am.		SX arr. pm.	dep. pm.
Newton Heath Shed	-	6.25LE			
Royton Jn.	6.50	7.18	Royton Jn.	-	2.45EBV
Shaw	7.28	-	Milnrow	3.5	3.35
			Shaw	3.55	-
		Shunt			
Shaw	-	8.27			Shunt
Milnrow	8.44	-	Shaw	-	6.30
			Royton Jn.	6.39	7.10LE
		Shunt	Rochdale	7.35	8.08
Milnrow	-	9.22	Moston Sidings	8.51	8.56LE
New Hey	9.29	-	Newton Heath Shed	9.01	-
		Shunt			
New Hey	-	10.09		SO	
Crompton Sidings	R	R	Royton Jn.	-	1.00LE
Shaw	R	R	Newton Heath Shed	1.18	-
Royton Jn.	10.27	-			

Shunt and test vacuum fitted vehicles

A fair gathering have assembled at the end of No 3 platform at Manchester Exchange to witness the presence of a summer Saturday extra. However, to the hardened enthusiast, a degree of mystery surrounds the photograph. No **52108** is a Newton Heath loco whilst 'Crab' 2-6-0 No **42789**, carrying Reporting Number W568 hails from Farnley Junction. A possibility is that the train originated from the Leeds/ Huddersfield area but where and why was the veteran 0-6-0 summoned for assistance? It may be that it was attached here at short notice whilst acting as Manchester Victoria West End Pilot - which would account for the lack of transfer of reporting number, (No 52108 carries a faint chalked inscription C622 from a previous working). Both locos are 'in the pink' and the train would almost certainly proceed over the former Central Division, probably to Blackpool - otherwise one would imagine a Patricroft engine at the head had it been destined for the North Wales coast. Perhaps the lady gricer amongst the throng has the answers.　　　　　　**2ND MAY 1959** ● **D. LAWRENCE**

Hurrying the breakdown train through Oldham Central is 0-6-0 No **52271**. Since their introduction in 1889 and throughout until 1960, an 'A' class was constantly deployed at the shed to attend to all manner of incidents at short notice. This was the last example and when No 52271 left for Lees (Oldham) in May 1961, Newton Heath bade farewell to to its final loco of L&Y origin. The crane is 30 ton No RS1075/30, built by Cowans Sheldon in 1943, which arrived from Rugby in 1954.　　　　　　**4TH APRIL 1959** ● **R. KEELEY**

No 52431 pilots Crewe North Class Five No 45390 on a returning holiday special from Llandudno between Royton Junction and Shaw. Bullcote Lane bridge was a favourite spot for photographers to record traffic on a summer Saturday which was invariably double headed.

23RD AUGUST 1958 ● B. HILTON

Engaged on shunting duties at Royton ▶ Junction is No 52328. Signs of dereliction are already in evidence - witness the collapse of an original L&Y rail built buffer stop and the encrusted grime on the privately owned 7 plank open wagon.

FEBRUARY 1955 ● G. WHITEHEAD

A familiar view from the ramp of Platform 11 at Manchester Victoria Station looking across towards East Junction Signalbox. No 52271 has the signal to proceed with parcels vans in the direction of the Cheetham Hill loop. Just in view through the gantry, left of the box are the Footbridge Down Fast Home and Cheetham Hill Down Fast Distants. These are part of a multiple junction signal and the Down Fast to Red Bank, just out of view, is likely to be 'off' to receive the short transfer to the sidings.

3RD FEBRUARY 1955 ● B.K.B. GREEN
▼

Two more pictures, again taken from Victoria's Platform 11 where so many of the class could be observed at work. Looking west, No **52139** brings freight through the middle line on a glorious Spring morning. Victoria West Junction Signalbox is visible as are the tracks diverging right away from the platform. These were used by local services to avoid having to pass through 11 Middle and Exchange Station.

1ST JUNE 1950 ● G. SHUTTLEWORTH

Looking in the opposite direction and Stanier 4-6-0 No **45624 *St. Helena*** arrives with a train of empty stock, possibly for Manchester Exchange. The presence of this Crewe North Jubilee would be popular with many spotters over on Platform 12, caught busily scribbling the number down. The leading Wallside Pilot is No **52161**, a long standing former Southport engine. Whilst it was usual to find a pair of these on duty by day, as many as four could be found during the night - occasionally working in tandem to assist the prodigious amount of freight traffic passing through in the early hours.

AUGUST 1958 ● J.A. COX

There is a real northern atmosphere within this panoramic view of Royton Junction Down Sidings. Terraced houses, allotments, pigeon sheds and a tried and trusted workhorse in the shape of ex L&Y 0-6-0 No **52275**, whose cab left the crew exposed to the elements. They were all a part of Lancashire life in the days of steam.　　　　**c1960 ● E.F. BENTLEY**

A local goods from Broadfield to Rochdale approaches Castleton North Junction behind 'A' Class No **52341**. The parcels van and wagons contain traffic from RAF 35MU but the loco was probably on loan to Bury shed. The early turn on Broadfield Pilot was a Newton Heath working who often used a borrowed B1. This was relieved by a Bury loco for the late turn and this train was part of that duty.

20TH JULY 1959 ● R.S. GREENWOOD

THE B1 CLASS 4-6-0s

At least two ex-LNER B1's were associated with the shed during the summer of 1950 *(see page 155 for details)*, but unfortunately it has not been possible to trace a photograph of No **61326**, the only one officially allocated. The loco arrived from Gorton on 11th August to replace another 39A engine, No 61223 which had been *on loan* during the previous month. It returned after a similar period but whether it displayed a 26A shedplate remains a mystery. No 61326 is approaching Guide Bridge with an express from Sheffield during the final winter of passenger steam operation on the former GC line.

JANUARY 1954 ● AUTHOR'S COLLECTION

THE BRITANNIA CLASS 4-6-2's

How the mighty had fallen! Spotlessly clean in ex-works condition, BR Standard Class 7 4-6-2 No **70000 *Britannia*** was unveiled in a blaze of glory at Liverpool Street Station in January 1951, having received a pair of newly cast nameplates in brass. This name had been transferred from the Newton Heath Jubilee No 45700 which, in turn, was later renamed *Amethyst*. The *Brits*, as they were commonly known, numbered 55 locomotives with the first members going to Stratford (London) and Norwich MPD's, primarily to work on the 2hr expresses between those two cities. Much has been recorded about their distinguished exploits over the ex GER line over the following decade, but the LMR and latterly the WR also achieved good results with them. Initially they were widespread - the SR had examples for working the prestigious *Golden Arrow* whilst others were at Polmadie (Glasgow) and Leeds (Holbeck). After being displaced from main line work, the majority gravitated to the LMR and in particular to Carlisle Kingmoor MPD which, by September 1966 had 33 examples. Not so No 70000 *Britannia*. After spells at Willesden, Crewe North and South, it arrived at Newton Heath in March 1966 in poor condition for two further months of work. On a clear day, the unkempt loco is pictured leaving Rochdale with a Brewery Sidings to Tees freight which turned out to be an inauspicious occasion. This was its last revenue earning duty in BR service, but fortunately it eventually survived in preservation.

8TH MAY 1966 ● **R.S. GREENWOOD**

On Friday 22nd July 1966, Driver Stan Tierney and Fireman George Bingham were asked to prepare 9F 2-10-0 No 92016 and then haul *Britannia* as far as Guide Bridge. This was the first stage of the loco's pilgrimage back to Stratford for a period of storage whilst awaiting a decision regarding its future. It was later vandalised and, as it was in a run down state anyway, was 'passed over' for official preservation in favour of No 70013 *Oliver Cromwell* which was in a much better condition. The *Britannia Loco Society* later rescued No 70000 and took it to the *Severn Valley Railway* where it was restored - but owing to axle loading restrictions, could only work between Bewdley and Kidderminster. The society then took the Pacific to the *Nene Valley Railway*, where (for a short period) external air brake equipment was fitted to enable the loco to haul the NVR's continental rolling stock. It then received a further overhaul for main line running, mostly between Crewe and Holyhead, but also over the Settle and Carlisle route. The loco was then sold to Pete Waterman and kept at *The Railway Age*, Crewe but has since been sold again to Jeremy Hosking. He intends to have it restored for further main line work at Crewe following a period as a static exhibit at the Barrow Hill roundhouse.

No 70048 *The Territorial Army 1908-1958* together with No 70045 *Lord Rowallan* were the first members to arrive, displaced from main line duties at Camden in January 1960. They were initially tried on the Glasgow turns but, despite their greater 7P power classification, proved to be no better than the Jubilees and tended to appear on secondary duties during their short stay. Initially Nos 70045-49 had gone new to Holyhead in May - August 1954 to work the Irish boat trains to and from Euston until November 1959 when the batch moved on to Crewe North. No 70048 passes Castleton South Junction with the 7.47am stopping train from Todmorden to Manchester Victoria.

12TH JULY 1960 ● **R.S. GREENWOOD**

The Sunday 9.20am Manchester Victoria to Blackpool Central was a typical duty. Although No **70045 *Lord Rowallan*** is showing Class A headlamps at St Annes-on-the-Sea, the train was all stations from Preston via the coast line, arriving nearly two hours later at 11.18am. The 'Brits' were rarely involved with the intensive services during the week. The tall lattice signal behind the train was locally known as the 'lighthouse', as a signalbox of that name was once situated there. **21ST FEBRUARY 1960 ● P. FITTON**

The 6.15pm Rochdale to Hellifield gets on its way behind No **70048 *The Territorial Army 1908-1958***. This working latterly produced a Newton Heath Class Five but always had Hellifield men on the footplate. **28TH JUNE 1960 ● R.S. GREENWOOD**

The second wave of Britannias arrived in July 1965 with Nos 70017 *Arrow*, 70021 *Morning Star*, 70034 *Thomas Hardy* and 70044 *Earl Haig* arriving en bloc from Crewe South. All four were in poor condition, bereft of nameplates and were used sparingly on fitted freight and parcels duties with occasional passenger work. No **70021 *Morning Star*** keeps a Model MGB waiting at Clayton Bridge level crossing as it slowly gets away with a Leeds bound parcels train.

NOVEMBER 1965 ● R. CORT

After a day's outing to the seaside, No **70017 *Arrow*** passes Weeton signalbox on its return to Manchester Victoria with the 7.12pm from Blackpool North.

5TH AUGUST 1965 ● P. FITTON

Another member with a returning Saturday Blackpool train shortly after transfer was No **70034 *Thomas Hardy*,** one mile south of Preston as the prominent maroon sign on Skew Bridge Signalbox indicates. Three of the Brits moved on to join the majority of the class at Carlisle Kingmoor, but No 70044 was withdrawn from Newton Heath in October 1966 and placed in store at Stockport Edgeley MPD. On Thursday 19th January 1967, Driver Len Goodchild and Fireman George Bingham prepared No 70034 which was visiting from Kingmoor. They then hauled Ivatt 2-6-0 No 46504 (withdrawn October 1966) to Crewe Works for cutting up and returned with EM1 electric loco No 26032 for Reddish.

17TH JULY 1965 ● R. FARRELL

The classic location for generations of photographers was here at Shap Wells. No **70045 *Lord Rowallan*** climbs towards the summit with an afternoon Manchester to Glasgow express. The loco's condition hardly inspired confidence and although signs of steam leakage are evident, the Pacific tackled thirteen bogies unaided. Salterwath Cottages, just visible in the background, were a pair occupied by Permanent Way staff during the LNWR and early LMS period. The Down line was temporarily held 'in possession' twice a year whilst they took delivery of a wagon load of coal from the local Tebay agent, shoveled out by hand. They were demolished in March 1968. During January 1966, *Lord Rowallan* became a Carlisle Kingmoor engine and whilst on shed had a slight altercation with another loco in the yard. Damage to the buffer beam resulted in the fitting of a pair of oval buffers, reputedly off a Duchess Pacific long since withdrawn.

AUGUST 1960 ● AUTHOR'S COLLECTION

A locomotive naming ceremony. Britannia Pacific No 70048 had been in service for ▶ four years before the large plates bearing the name ***The Territorial Army 1908-1958*** were unveiled on 23rd July 1958 at London Euston Station by the Duke of Norfolk. It was the only member of the class whose plates were cast in aluminium and came complete with red background. **23RD JULY 1958 ● AUTHOR'S COLLECTION**

The intensive Blackpool to Manchester service offered work for the loco before its transfer away in September 1961. No **70048 *The Territorial Army 1908 1958*** makes a spirited departure from Leyland station. **1ST JULY 1961 ● I.G. HOLT**
▼

THE STANDARD 2-6-4 TANKS

Departing from Oldham Central in bright sunlight with a Manchester Victoria to Rochdale train is Standard 2-6-4T No **80093**. The view is from the adjoining platforms of Oldham Clegg Street which served trains operating over the former Oldham, Ashton and Guide Bridge line. Immediately right of No 80093's front buffer beam is a signal post and fitting but with its stop arm missing. This was the 'Wakes Week' signal brought into use for a fortnight each year to enable additional line capacity to be achieved between Oldham Werneth and Mumps Signalboxes - such was the intensity of traffic. The necessary arm was installed and connected on the post whilst the vital piece of mechanical interlocking was inserted in the Mumps lever frame. At the end of the holiday period, the signal arm and interlocking were carefully removed and stowed away in the Signal Locking Fitters Shop at the nearby Oldham Central Signal and Telegraph Depot ready for another year.   **c1956** ● **J. DAVENPORT**

Bunker first away from Kearsley Station with a Manchester Victoria to Bolton local is No **80060**. The train is about to pass through the 295 yard long Farnworth Tunnel and after further stops at Farnworth & Halshaw Moor and Moses Gate Stations, the 11 mile journey will have taken 28 minutes. The cooling towers of Kearsley Power Station dominate behind the building on the Up platform.

c1956 ● **AUTHOR'S COLLECTION**

An interesting working was the Saturdays Only Manchester Victoria to Crewe Parcels which ran via Rochdale and Oldham. No **80044** is caught performing the task at New Barn Lane, Rochdale. This particular example was one of only 24 of the 999 BR Standard locos cut up by British Railways in their own scrapyards, in this case Crewe Works.　　　　**4TH JULY 1959** ● **R.S. GREENWOOD**

The small cotton manufacturing town of Royton was served by a short branch from the Junction Station of the same name - much akin as to that at nearby Middleton. The single platform, capable of accommodating a train of 8 coaches, was flanked by goods sidings and an impressive cotton warehouse which overshadowed the station. Having run around its train, No **80052** is awaiting departure, returning to Manchester Victoria via Oldham. The Standard tanks shared the local passenger work with the Fairburn and Stanier variety during the mid 1950s until their transfer away. Goods services were curtailed in 1964 and full closure came two years later.

c1955 ● **R. CARPENTER COLLECTION**

The Middleton Branch by comparison had a limited goods facility but a station which possessed both arrival and departure platforms. Standard 2-6-4T No **80053** stands near the stop blocks with a train from Manchester. It will shortly propel the empty stock out of the platform before running round and placing the formation on the Up side. On 11th March 1953, when barely 4 months old, this particular loco came to grief at Oldham Central when it ran into a Lees 'Breadvan', No 40059 whilst working the 1.00pm Manchester Victoria to Rochdale train. It had been the last of a batch of five (Nos 80049-53) which arrived new from Brighton in November/December 1952. They were joined by a similar number from Bury (February 1956) for a short period before the first ones moved on to Chester. By May 1960 all ten were transferred to the Scottish Region in a bid to standardise class allocation.

MARCH 1954 ● **AUTHOR'S COLLECTION**

A generous covering of snow welcomed in the New Year of 1962. The public holiday fell on a Monday - but it was work as usual for the crew of WD No **90561.** The lengthy train of returning mineral empties from Middleton Junction to the Yorkshire coalfield climbs the last few chains on the approach to Summit tunnel. **1ST JANUARY 1962 ● R.S. GREENWOOD**

THE WD CLASS 2-8-0's

An Up mixed freight for Crewe passes through the the leafy suburbs of Cheadle Hulme behind No **90568,** whose front number appears on both smokebox door and buffer beam. The small property adjacent to the railway is the original station building which was named 'Cheadle'. It opened on 10th May 1842 but closed shortly afterwards when new passenger facilities were developed at the junction with the Macclesfield line. The larger building, partially hidden, was the original Station Master's house. The connecting footbridge and splitting signal are just visible beyond the train. **15TH SEPTEMBER 1951 ● B.K.B. GREEN**

The WD 2-8-0 locos were engaged in all manner of work over the Central Division. No **90289** has clear signals to proceed through Oldham Clegg Street and on to the OA&GB with a train of empty stock - but the class could equally be found on excursion traffic when Newton Heath was desperate for suitable motive power. This particular example was supplied by the North British Locomotive Co. Ltd. The tracks to the left served the adjacent Oldham Central Station beyond which stands Mumps No 1 signal-box with part of the town's Central Gas Works also in view.

AUGUST 1954 ● J. DAVENPORT

26A Austerities were rarely observed in the West Midlands south of Crewe, so it came as a surprise to find WD 2-8-0 No **90390** passing under the newly erected catenary at Ashton, Northamptonshire, south of Roade, with a mixed freight.

12TH SEPTEMBER 1963 ● K. FAIREY

A train of empty mineral wagons has just passed under Alfred Street Bridge, Bury at 12.05pm behind WD 2-8-0 No **90291**. The loco is working hard but needs no assistance on the climb up the 1 in 85 Broadfield Bank towards Heap Bridge Junction.

23RD DECEMBER 1961 ● E.F. BENTLEY

Having skirted around the outside of the train shed at Shrewsbury Station, WD 2-8-0 No **90530** awaits the calling on signal with a southbound ICI ammonia tank train. Most of the freight heading north went forward between Platforms 1 and 2 on the through road. The loco's presence in the area is unusual but equally surprising was its later transfer to Patricroft (with No 90222) in February 1960 helping to provide the ex-LNWR depot with representatives for the first time.　　　**16TH AUGUST 1958 ● B. MORRISON**

Heading home towards Lancashire is No 90523 with a train of coal. The location is Whitehall Junction, Leeds and it is passing the site of Holbeck Low Level Station. The lattice girder bridge carries the ex-GN main line from Leeds Central to Wakefield Westgate and beyond and just in view on the far left is one of Copley Hill's A1 Pacifics reversing down to the terminus prior to departure with a London Kings Cross express.　　　**MAY 1960 ● R. FARRELL**

The 1.00pm SX Bolton to Royton Junction Class F passes Bury Gas Works Sidings with No **90248** at the helm. The WD 2-8-0s were regularly engaged on all manner of transfer freight in the Manchester area and often visited the other local sheds. On the afternoon of Monday, 22nd April 1963, No 90248 found itself on Trafford Park MPD in the company of an equally dirty shedmate, Jubilee 4-6-0 No 45635 *Tobago*. Manchester United were playing Wolverhampton Wanderers that evening and the pair were hastily borrowed for Footex duties. This involved shuttling supporters between Manchester Central Station and the wooden platform alongside the Old Trafford stadium both before and after a game in which United won 2 - 1.

28TH FEBRUARY 1963 ● E.F. BENTLEY

In December 1950, some twelve WD 2-8-0s were transferred from the Western Region to Newton Heath in exchange for the equivalent number of Stanier 2-8-0s. Most of these went to 87K (Swansea Victoria) for work over the Central Wales line to Shrewsbury but six months later, another nine WD's began to arrive off the Southern Region including this one, No **90669**. The loco has passed through New Hey with empty stock to form the 4.00pm Shaw to Blackpool North excursion. The leading coaches are of ex-Midland vintage.

17TH AUGUST 1957 ● B. HILTON

A familiar location on the West Coast Main Line, south of Preston is Farington Junction. In typically shabby external condition, No **90163** is in charge of a Permanent Way train on the Up Fast - the empty bolster wagons suggesting that it may well be returning to Castleton via Bolton and Bury. The loco was a relatively early casualty, being withdrawn in December 1962 after having arrived with the closure of nearby Belle Vue MPD in March 1956. Away over the fields is the unmistakable shape of the coal hopper belonging to Lostock Hall MPD.

**10TH SEPTEMBER 1962 ●
B.W.L. BROOKSBANK**

The class were regularly employed on much of the freight work from the Manchester yards to Gowhole Sidings, nearly two miles south of New Mills South Junction. Traffic was routed via Midland Junction, Ashburys, Reddish and Marple and it was common to see as many as five 26A WD's operating by day over the route in the 1950s. No **90715** has reached Strines Station with a train of tarpaulined wagons for Gowhole and is about to pass under the elegant Midland pattern lattice footbridge, dating from 1884. The station, situated between Marple and New Mills, is somewhat remote from the local community but convenient for the textile print works served by a small goods yard.

1962 ● **J. CLARKE**

A returning train from Gowhole has been routed from Romiley Junction via Woodley and Hyde Central. No **90328** is passing through the platforms of Hyde North station before joining the electrified Manchester to Sheffield line as far as Ashburys Junction.

18TH AUGUST 1962 ● **E.F. BENTLEY**

Passing through Hindley with a Down freight is No **90388**. Close detection will reveal a miniature snowplough fitted to this loco (and also to No 90338) which were drilled out in the 'Parlour' specifically for the purpose.

4TH NOVEMBER 1961 ● J.A. SOMMERFIELD

Another rail train which is loose coupled is in the hands of WD 2-8-0 No **90366**, piloting one of the Stanier variety, Kirkby-in-Ashfield's No **48102**. The destination is Castleton Permanent Way Depot and the location, Bury Loop Junction.

21ST FEBRUARY 1960 ● R. FARRELL

The passing time at Bradkirk signalbox was 12.22pm for No **90390** hauling a Down coal train for Fleetwood Power Station. This was unusual as the WD's observed here tended to be Rose Grove examples working from the Burnley coalfield.

6TH OCTOBER 1962 ● P. FITTON

Approaching Rochdale Station from the east with an Up coal train is No **90105**, whilst Jubilee 4-6-0 No **45717 *Dauntless*** departs with the premier train of the day, the 10.30am Liverpool Exchange to Newcastle restaurant car express. *Dauntless* was a Newton Heath engine before its transfer away to Bank Hall, via Southport, in October 1948.　　　**1ST NOVEMBER 1958** ● **R.S. GREENWOOD**

▲

Trundling through Castleton and passing under Manchester Road bridge with freight signalled for the Heywood Branch is No **90390**. Newton Heath had no fewer than 33 WD's on the books at this time.　　**28TH MAY 1960** ● **R.S. GREENWOOD**

◄ **Another WD involved in Gowhole traffic** is No **90561**. The loco is caught opposite New Mills South Junction signalbox on the Up Slow line approaching the marshalling yard.

c1963 ● **AUTHOR'S COLLECTION**

The splitting signal at Castleton South Junction shows the home arm off in the Castleton East Junction direction. The train is a Brewery Sidings to Rochdale local transfer with 2-8-0 No **90289** in charge.   **26TH SEPTEMBER 1959** ● **R.S. GREENWOOD**

An unusual view of WD No 90222 at Royton. During September 1964, the remaining three locos, Nos 90516/20 and 90718 moved away to Aintree by which time sufficient Stanier 8Fs and Standard 9Fs had arrived to satisfy most freight requirements.

FEBRUARY 1955 ● **G. WHITEHEAD**

A bizarre combination of motive power. The SSO Morecambe to Manchester Victoria was extended to Oldham at the end of their Wakes week and changed locos at Manchester Victoria. The shed had to resort to a pair of 8F's on this occasion - Austerity No **90376** piloting Stanier No **48553**. The train has become empty stock and is near Jubilee crossing on its way to Lightbowne.   **25TH JUNE 1960** ● **R.S. GREENWOOD**

THE 9F CLASS 2-10-0's

BR Standard Class 9 2-10-0 No 92022, originally fitted with an ill fated Franco-Crosti boiler, leaves Patricroft Sidings with the 9.47am cross-Manchester transfer freight to Brewery Sidings. By the time Nos 92022 and 92026 arrived at Newton Heath (June and September 1964), they had been converted to steam in the conventional manner. Patricroft's 'New' shed yard is partially visible behind the train whilst an 0-6-0 diesel shunter is also in evidence. The freshly ballasted track curving away to the right are the lines to Monton. This fine photograph was taken by signalman and steam enthusiast Tony Oldfield from Patricroft North Sidings box.   **JUNE 1965** ● **J.A. OLDFIELD**

The 9F 2-10-0s were another class which came to Newton Heath largely by default. Five members, Nos 92015/6/7 and 92161/2 were the first arrivals - initially on loan from the Midland Division w/e 28th June 1958. They were to be used on fitted freights on weekdays and passenger trains on Saturdays. Their arrival coincided with a decision to install long welded rails on main lines as and when they needed replacing. The consequences of this were four new welding depots, one locally at Castleton with others at Dinsdale (Darlington), Hookagate (Shrewsbury) and Motherwell. Chesterton Junction (Cambridge) and Redbridge (Southampton) being the two existing sites. The 9Fs were frequently observed leaving Castleton on this traffic to all manner of destinations. Making good progress on the slow line south of Leyland is No **92016** with a pair of bolster wagons behind the tender as part of an express freight.   **5TH SEPTEMBER 1964** ● **R. FARRELL**

One of the first weekend passenger turns was entrusted to No **92161** which, although showing Reporting Number C778, it is displaying headlamps indicating a train of empty stock which will obviously form an excursion further down the line, starting out from a Lancashire town - perhaps Chorley. The 9F is about to pass over Lostock Troughs, 3 miles north west of Bolton but the facility is of little value since the class were not fitted with water pick up equipment. The tender's capacity (approx 4,750 gallons) however was more than adequate to reach its required destination.

4TH MAY 1958 ● D. HAMPSON

On Sunday, 29th June 1958 shortly after arrival, the shed had a couple of excursions to the North Wales coast and the Running Foreman, after consultation, earmarked two of the 9F's for these jobs, much to the consternation of the drivers. "Treat them as Class Fives and tell the firemen to keep the back corners well filled" was the advice given. No 92017 handled a Castleton to Llandudno excursion which was made up of a 10 coach set of green liveried Southern stock (No 938). This had arrived at Lightbowne Sidings the previous evening off an Eastbourne to Oldham Relief worked by No 45697 *Achilles* of Carlisle Kingmoor. Two trouble free trips resulted and the 'Spaceships', as they were known, soon became accepted and, indeed, popular locos on the Central Division. No **92015** - looking worse for wear, brings a mixed goods along the Up Slow line, south of Preston.

12TH SEPTEMBER 1963 ● F. DEAN

Caught running on the Down Slow line at Kirkham with yet another Blackpool bound excursion is a very presentable No **92017**. As well as handling holiday traffic, the 9F's also regularly worked the Isle of Man boat trains to Fleetwood during this period.

9TH JULY 1960 ● P. FITTON

Holyrood Street bridge, which overlooked the railway at the south end of Royton Station, was a popular vantage point for local photographers. A Rhyl bound excursion passes through behind No **92017** towards Oldham Mumps from where it will pass through Clegg Street and take the OA&GB line to Ashton Moss. The 9Fs were ultimately banished from traversing the Oldham Loop owing to axle loading restrictions, however in view of their success on other routes, a permanent transfer was confirmed w/e 13th September 1958

14TH SEPTEMBER 1958 ● B. HILTON

A panoramic view of the Derbyshire hills forms the perfect backdrop for the R.C.T.S. 'East Midlander No 9 Railtour' at Chinley. No **92077** and 8 coaches of LMS corridor stock are en route back to Nottingham Midland having earlier visited Crewe Works. The outward journey was via Beeston, Castle Donington, Burton-on-Trent, Tamworth High Level, Water Orton, Walsall, Wolverhampton, Stafford, Wellington, Market Drayton and Crewe Works Yard. Whilst the party visited the works, No 92077 retired to South shed for servicing. The Railtour then returned via Acton Grange, Arpley, Latchford, Skelton Junction, Heaton Mersey, Stockport Tiviot Dale, Romiley and New Mills South Junction. The train continued over the Peak to Ambergate, Codnor Park and back to Nottingham Midland.

21ST MAY 1966 ● M.S. WELCH

A classic case of being in the right place at the right time! Whilst cameraman Peter Fitton was busy calculating his exposure of No **92080** plodding stealthily along with a Down mixed freight, suddenly Rebuilt Patriot No **45527** *Southport* bursts on to the scene, overtaking with the Down 'Lakes Express'. The location is Skew Bridge, 1 mile south of Preston, as the large sign affixed to the base of the signalbox in the distance always reminded us.

8TH AUGUST 1964 ● P. FITTON

2-10-0 No 92022 brings a mineral train through Castleton towards Moston Exchange Sidings. Between June and October 1964, no fewer than fourteen 9F's arrived off the Midland Division where they were deemed surplus to requirements. The other Crosti boilered engine, No 92026 had already gone to Birkenhead in May 1965 and nine months later this engine followed on to Merseyside, but went to Speke Junction.

SEPTEMBER 1965 ● R. FARRELL

One of these arrivals, No 92080 passes Stalybridge No 2 signalbox heading east with a lengthy bolster train. The 15B - Kettering shedplate previously carried by this engine had been correctly replaced by a 9D plate which were becoming rarities. By this time it was standard practice for all new arrivals to have the code painted directly on to the smokebox door, although standards of execution varied considerably.

8TH JUNE 1965 ● G. COLTAS

One of the original five, No 92162 works a train from St. Helens Junction on a bright summer's morning over the ex LNWR lines between Eccles Junction and station on the approaches to Ordsall Lane. Although nearby Patricroft MPD never had any on allocation, they were common visitors to the area.

AUGUST 1961 ● J.R. CARTER

The Castleton East Junction Home and Station Distant signals are off allowing 9F No **92017** to proceed through the platforms with empty stock for Todmorden. After turning the nine coach train on the triangle there, it then formed a half day excursion bound for Southport via Rochdale and Bolton. The 2-10-0's tended to be used more sparingly on passenger workings over the Central Division in later years.

18TH JUNE 1960 ● R.S. GREENWOOD

A regular 9F working over the Settle and Carlisle line was the Carlisle Durran Hill to Oldham Glodwick Road empty van train. Passing between Hellifield North Junction signal box and the sandhouse, attached to the rear of Hellifield MPD, is a commendably clean No **92162**. The train would draw to a stand in the platform where a Newton Heath crew were rostered to relieve their Kingmoor counterparts.

13TH MAY 1961 ● **R.S. GREENWOOD**

Approaching Bury Knowsley Street Station with the train and seen crossing the Irwell viaduct at Elton is sister engine No **92161**. This attractive Victorian structure still spans the river, canal and Wellington Road. It was rare to find a 9F on Longsight shed but the loco was borrowed by 9A on July 26th 1958 for the 9.00am (SO) Manchester London Road to Penzance which it worked as far as Shrewsbury. It returned with the 10.30am (SO) Paignton - Manchester. In May 1965 it left for Kingmoor, whose locos remained almost daily visitors to 26A (9D by that time) right up to Kingmoor's closure on 30th December 1967. No 92161 revisited its old haunts on at least three occasions, 13th August, 17th October and 9th November 1966 before withdrawal in December 1966.   **8TH FEBRUARY 1960** ● **R. FARRELL**

Emerging from Bradshawgate Tunnel and passing Byng Street carriage Sidings is No **92162**, about to pass through Bolton Trinity Street Station with the empty van train. Prominent on the skyline, overlooking the junction with the Bolton avoiding line towards Lostock Junction, are the Kings Hall buildings. The approach to Oldham by this train was by a somewhat circuitous route via Manchester Victoria and Ashton.

13TH JULY 1962 ● **D. HAMPSON**

▲

After its passenger outing with the 'East Midlander' Railtour, it was a return to the old order for No **92077**, slogging away with mineral wagons back and forth on the Calder Valley line. No longer in pristine condition, the 9F has a train of empties destined for Healey Mills and is approaching Mirfield, having just passed Heaton Lodge Junction. In the distance, beyond the engine's exhaust is Battyeford girder bridge which carries the LNWR 'New Line' to Leeds over the River Calder. A transfer to Carnforth in March 1967 eventually resulted in it being one of only three (Nos 92160/7 were the others) which survived until the very end of steam.

12TH JANUARY 1967 ● G. COLTAS

▲

A motive power shortage in the area in October 1963 brought about the unlikely transfer of a further three 9Fs from former GWR depots. No **92208** (ex-Cardiff East Dock) blasts through Romiley with a short freight for Gowhole. The others were Nos 92233 and 92249 from Ebbw Junction.

25TH JANUARY 1964 ● G. WHITEHEAD

◄ **The final 9F arrival was the most short lived.** Double Chimneyed No **92247** arrived from Banbury in September 1966 and was promptly withdrawn the following month. It was fortunately caught in action passing Mirfield Shed with a mixed freight.

22ND SEPTEMBER 1966 ● G. COLTAS

A Saturday morning freight from Brewery Sidings to Royton Junction approaches Castleton Sidings behind 9F No **92161**. The conveyance of livestock - as is the case with the leading wagon - as part of a mixed train, met with stringent legislation. A person responsible for transit would usually travel in the Guard's van, making sure that the forwarding station or exchange point would have been duly notified in advance.

27TH FEBRUARY 1960 ● R.S. GREENWOOD

Leaving Preston heading for Skew Bridge and the south with an empty bogie bolster train, possibly bound for Castleton, is No **92016**.

AUGUST 1966 ● J. HAMMOND

Three of the original allocation spent a turbulent three month period 'up the road' at Bolton before returning home. The locos, Nos 92015/6/7 went there in September 1962, primarily to work the 8.20pm Bolton to Moston freight followed by the late evening Ancoats to Heysham fitted freight. No **92016** would appear to be the only regular performer with the other two being stopped on shed for lengthy periods for a variety of reasons. By 22nd December they had been replaced by Class Fives, Nos 45156 *The Ayrshire Yeomanry,* (Bolton's one and only named locomotive), 45224 and 45232 which had both been at 26A since LMS days. Later in the 1960s - No 92016 passes through Lancaster Castle Station with a train of empty stock whilst Fireman Alan Bedford is caught taking a breather!

4TH AUGUST 1966 ● R. FARRELL

Although Class D11 4-4-0s Nos 62662 *Prince of Wales* & 62664 *Princess Mary* were never allocated to the depot, they qualify for inclusion as both locomotives were sent to 26A some days prior to a railtour for crew familiarisation purposes and worked several trains over the Central Division. The former Great Central engines were both from Northwich MPD (8E) with *Princess Mary* being first to arrive on 30th April 1956, ex-Gorton Works whilst *Prince of Wales* made its way on 6th May. No 62664 awaits the signal at Victoria Station before proceeding tender first to Newton Heath, having previously worked the 9.15am Leeds City to Manchester Exchange

4TH MAY 1956 ● B. ROBERTS

The '**Pennine Pullman**' was a 440 mile round trip from London Marylebone to Kings Cross, supposedly the longest enthusiasts' day railtour organised in Britain at the time. A4 Pacific No 60014 *Silver Link* worked to Sheffield Victoria before handing over to EM2 No 27002. Nos **62662 *Prince of Wales* & 62664 *Princess Mary*** then went forward from Midland Junction (Manchester) to Rotherwood via Rochdale and Mirfield after which *Silver Link* returned to the capital. The duo are seen approaching Moston Station, passing through the reputedly 'dreary cutting', immortalised by Ewan McColl. Notice the two young boys watching from a catwalk over Thirlmere aqueduct.

12TH MAY 1956 ● J. DAVENPORT

There was a scheduled stop at Rochdale at 3.11pm by which time a number of enthusiasts had assembled at the north end of Platform 1. Whilst most of the gathering are admiring the engines - the gricer, looking suspiciously at the camera and dressed in typical 1950s attire, has a cherished possession in his jacket pocket - an Ian Allan Combined Volume! **12TH MAY 1956 ● J.A. COX**

Some of No 62664 Princess Mary's activities prior to the railtour were as follows:

3rd/4th/5th May 1956
6.02am Greenfield - Huddersfield. 7.04am Huddersfield - Leeds City. 9.15am (SX), 9.20am (SO) Leeds City - Manchester Exchange. *On 4th May also worked:* 5.35pm Manchester Victoria - Todmorden. 8.10pm Todmorden - Mytholmroyd frt. 9.18pm Mytholmroyd - Rochdale frt.

7th May 1956
8.35am Manchester Victoria - Blackburn. LE Bolton. 1pm Bolton - Royton Jct frt.

8th May 1956
7pm Mytholmroyd - Stockport parcels.

Rarely did one see a Bank Hall Jubilee running with a pilot whilst operating over the ex L&Y system. No **45719** *Glorious* has a Newton Heath Fairburn 2-6-4 tank No **42280** for company whilst passing through Castleton Station with an eastbound express composed partly of a scratch set of Gresley stock. Whether the engine was detached at Rochdale remains unrecorded.

9TH JULY 1960 ● R.S.GREENWOOD

It was more common to observe double heading on the West Coast Main line. Class Five 4-6-0 No **45220** has Warrington's unrebuilt Patriot No **45550** inside as the pair enter Lancaster Castle Station with a southbound express. The Newton Heath engine came off at Preston.

1960 ● K. FAIREY

A Scarborough bound excursion has another 26A Class Five 4-6-0 acting as pilot loco. No **45102** and Standard Class Five No **73163** of York MPD form an unusual combination. The location is near Kirkham Abbey, between York and Malton.

AUGUST 1958 ● AUTHOR'S COLLECTION

A Manchester Victoria to Southport train has the luxury of two engines passing through Wigan. Stanier 2-6-4T No **42644** from the town's former L&Y depot is piloting No **45224** and is approaching Wigan Wallgate. The West Coast Main Line crosses in the foreground.
28TH MAY 1960 ● **R.J. FARRELL**

▲

The Scotswood to Red Bank empty van train produced an incredible permutation of locomotives and classes. Two from Newton Heath are in charge on this occasion. A low sun nicely highlights Unrebuilt Patriot No **45503** *The Royal Leicestershire Regiment* piloting Crab 2-6-0 No **42707** passing through Castleton.

9TH SEPTEMBER 1958 ● **R.S. GREENWOOD**

Jubilee 4-6-0 No 45635 *Tobago* has ▶ unusual front end assistance in the form of Holyhead Class Five No **45429**. The pair are beginning the assault on Shap with a Manchester - Glasgow train. The ex-works condition of the Class Five suggests that it might be on a running in turn.

1959 ● **J. DAVENPORT**

Passing Diggle Junction with an express from Newcastle to Liverpool Lime Street are Class Five No **44891** and one of the last Royal Scots to survive in unrebuilt form, No **46156 *The South Wales Borderer*** of Edge Hill MPD. The Class Five, working back to Newton Heath from the Leeds area, would detach at Manchester Exchange, thus saving the path of a light engine movement, which was common practice. A Fowler Class 7F 0-8-0 No **49548** also stands at the throat of the Up sidings whilst working one of the Lees (Oldham) trip workings. The loco was withdrawn the following July. ▶

AUGUST 1950 ● J. DAVENPORT

Similar circumstances may be the reason for this combination of Class Five No **45202** and Patricroft Jubilee No **45645 *Collingwood.*** The train is again the 10.05am ex-Newcastle and the location is Thornhill LNW Junction, east of Mirfield, with the Power Station prominent. The locomotives' exhaust obscures Ravensthorpe Station, situated immediately beyond the junction, serving the Leeds line only. The quadruple track trailing in on the right is the Calder Valley route towards Wakefield and the section from here to Mirfield Junction was originally jointly owned by the rival LNW and L&Y Companies.

JULY 1958 ● J. DAVENPORT

'This is Crewe - This is Crewe'. The three words constantly uttered by the station announcer - but the multitude of gricers who made a regular pilgrimage to their mecca needed no reminding. The arrival of No **45700 *Amethyst*** off the Chester line would be met by mixed emotions. The Manchester contingent might utter howls of derision, but for many it was a rare Jubilee, a cop, a reason for mild celebration and one of the highlights of their day. Loud cheers were usually reserved for a Polmadie Duchess from the north - such was the unique atmosphere at Crewe on those summer Saturdays. Three days earlier, No 45700 had come off the works having received its last Heavy General overhaul and one of its running in turns was acting pilot to Class Five No **45026** on the 1.20pm Llandudno to Derby (between Chester and Crewe). Unfortunately signs of impending electrification are present and the halcyon days would soon be but a memory.

19TH JULY 1958 ● B.W.L. BROOKSBANK

▼

The summer season generally reached a climax with the commencement of the Oldham Wakes Holiday period. For instance by Friday lunchtime, 20th June 1952, the depot had to have no fewer than 61 locos available ready to handle all the extra traffic and have a plentiful supply of coal. This included 34 trains which departed from the Oldham district alone. The first engine went off shed later that afternoon to pick up stock for the longer distance overnight specials which mainly headed south and accounted for 11 locos. Newton Heath's own Class Fives and Jubilees which were known to be in good working order were generally used. The 23 extras from Oldham that followed on Saturday were subjected to whatever motive power was left on shed - often WD 2-8-0's! Even the pilot locos around the Oldham Loop were visitors. Such a combination is approaching New Hey with yet another seaside special as 4F 0-6-0 No **44214** from Derby pilots Jubilee 4-6-0 No **45642 Boscawen.**

16TH JUNE 1962 ● R.S. GREENWOOD

A similar combination with an Oldham bound excursion on the OA&GB line near Park Bridge. The pilot 4F 0-6-0 is another stranger from Midland territory - Burton-on-Trent's No **44332.** The train engine is long standing Jubilee No **45635 Tobago.** Both locos are working hard up the gradient past Snipe Clough on the last leg of the journey. The train is full of returning holidaymakers from Llandudno - hence the Western Division Reporting Number W473. After depositing them at Oldham Clegg Street and Central, both locos will continue with the empty stock around the loop via Rochdale, Castleton, Middleton Junction and Moston before arriving at Lightbowne Sidings, Newton Heath.

JUNE 1953 ● J. DAVENPORT

In its day, the celebrated Scotswood (Newcastle) to Red Bank (Manchester) empty parcels vans produced, arguably, the most unpredictable variety of motive power on a daily basis observed anywhere on the BR network. A train whose length averaged 20 bogie vehicles, was invariably double headed by two mixed traffic or passenger locomotives between York and Red Bank. When production of the *Daily Mirror* moved to Manchester in November 1955, an extra train - the 12.05am to Newcastle was introduced with the empty vans (plus others) then returning on a daily basis. Newton Heath's engines featured prominently over the years as on this occasion when a named B1 from York, No **61018 Gnu** is caught piloting No **45716 Swiftsure.** With the rear half of the train still on the viaduct, the pair make a fine spectacle sweeping through the platforms at Todmorden Station.

13TH APRIL 1964 ● R.S. GREENWOOD

The depot had a brief association with the ex-LNER B1 4-6-0's during the summer of 1950. No **61223** had been loaned from neighbouring Gorton between 2nd July and 11th August, supposedly for crew familiarisation. It was then relieved by No 61326 which was officially transferred until the onset of the winter timetable thus becoming the one and only ex-LNER locomotive to be allocated. Newton Heath men frequently relieved their counterparts from Sheffield Darnall and other depots at Midland Junction with westbound excursion traffic. There may have possibly been a similar arrangement the previous year. Official LNER transfer records show Nos 61225 and 61109, again both Gorton locos, being transferred away to the LMR for short periods (29th May 1949 to 5th June 1949 and 3rd July to 17th July respectively). Unfortunately the moves to where are not recorded within the LMR records - but it seems likely that Newton Heath was the recipient. No 61223 has the company of Carlisle Upperby Class Five No **45439** on the 7pm Manchester Victoria to Blackpool service. The train has just cleared Agecroft Junction with the pilot engine possibly saving a path from an unbalanced working.

12TH JULY 1950 ● **C.A. APPLETON**

Empty carriage stock from Stockport (Edgeley) to Oldham Mumps passes Castleton Sidings, Rochdale behind Ivatt 2-6-0 No **46487** and Jubilee 4-6-0 No **45702 Colossus.** This was a common combination of class observed round the Oldham Loop on excursion traffic during the 1950's and early 1960's.

24TH JUNE 1961 ● **I.G. HOLT**

Rugby League's annual showpiece was doubtless the Challenge Cup Final, played at London's Wembley Stadium and the occasion offered fans from the towns of Lancashire and Yorkshire a day out, irrespective of who was playing. The vast majority of the crowd, which averaged 90,000 in the 1950s, were folk from 'up north'. Two Newton Heath locos are again in tandem, in charge of an Oldham 'Green Final' excursion at Heyside. Starting out from Werneth, the pilot engine, Stanier Class 4 2-6-4T No **42620** will drop off at Rochdale East Junction leaving Class Five No **45336** to complete the journey. The volume of extra traffic descending on the capital that Saturday lunchtime was awesome. The loco would be serviced at either Willesden, Neasden or Cricklewood depending on where the stock was to be stabled during the match. For the record Widnes beat Hull Kingston Rovers 13 - 5 in front of 84,488 spectators.

9TH MAY 1964 ● **D. CASH**

A trio of Newton Heath locos at work! A combination of unusually clean Class Fives, Nos **45202** (pilot) and **45220** make haste through Castleton towards Middleton Junction with the Scotswood - Red Bank empty vans. Much earlier in the day, No 45220 had worked the 12.05am 'News' through to Newcastle with a crew change at York. After servicing at Gateshead MPD, it worked back to York piloting a Heaton loco on the 6.56am passenger from Newcastle (the loco used on Tuesdays often worked back with the Inverness - York car sleeper) before retiring to Clifton shed. The returning empty vans arrived at York in the early afternoon, usually behind a Heaton V2 or, on occasions a B1 or Pacific engine before being relieved by the Class Five together with, on this occasion, No 45202 which had arrived earlier on an unbalanced freight working. The train was due to depart at 2.41pm but was prone to late running. It was York MPD's responsibility for providing the motive power for this second leg and Newton Heath engines often featured. Meanwhile, approaching on the Down line is Fowler 7F No **49508** with eastbound freight from Brewery Sidings.

13TH APRIL 1964 ● R.S. GREENWOOD

DIESEL SHUNTERS

Lastly, it must be acknowledged that although Newton Heath MPD had been closely associated with a variety of diesel engines and their workings, it is only those of the shunting variety that were ever allocated to the depot, both during and after the days of steam. The records of the summer of 1959 shows BR English Electric 0-6-0's Nos D3588-92 as being first to arrive but others soon followed. An unidentified member passes the shed transferring freight from Moston to Brewery Sidings. Heading eastbound with coal is the now preserved 8F, No **48773**. Meanwhile, a visitor from Birkenhead, No **92069** makes its way slowly to St. Mary's Road turntable after replenishing its tender.

JUNE 1965 ● E. HUMPHREY

Twenty diminutive 0-4-0 diesel hydraulic shunters (Nos D2850 - D2869) were introduced by the Yorkshire Engine Company in 1960. Newton Heath took delivery of five and one could then be found outstationed at Oldham Clegg Street Parcels Concentration Depot during the week, returning for servicing at weekend. No **D2858** rests between duties in its modern surroundings.

25TH JANUARY 1961 ● G. WHITEHEAD

LOCOMOTIVE ALLOCATIONS

The following tables cover the entire BR period from 1st January 1948 (the first day of Nationalisation) until the depot's closure to steam on 1st July 1968. Certain Pre-Grouping locos which survived the early period have been credited with their BR numbers, although in some cases did not carry them. Photographs of locos illustrated in the book are cross-referenced by page number in the first column. *Indicates loco withdrawn from Newton Heath MPD. The period on allocation is represented by: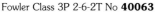

Fowler Class 3P 2-6-2T No **40063**

LMS Class 2P 4-4-0 No **M682**

Fairburn Class 4P 2-6-4T No **42289**

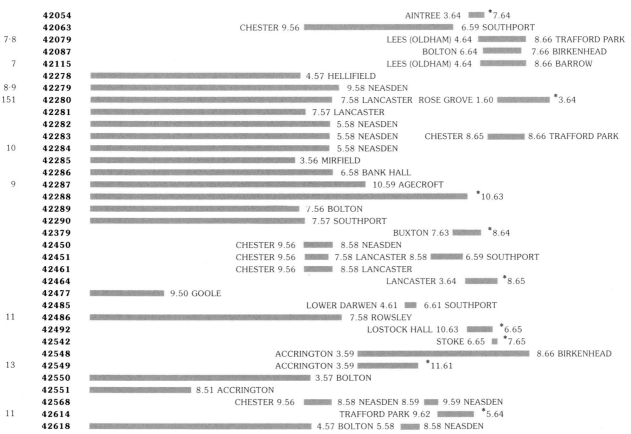

PAGE   **1948** ——————————————————————————————————➤ **1968**

CLASS 3P 2-6-2T

PAGE	No	Allocation
5	40013	▬▬▬▬▬▬▬ *12.59
3·4	40014	LEES (OLDHAM) 9.55 ▬▬▬▬▬ *5.60
3·4·6	40015	▬▬▬▬▬▬▬ *3.61
5	40062	LEES (OLDHAM) 9.55 ▬▬▬▬ *11.60
4·6	40063	▬▬▬▬▬▬▬ *8.62
	40065	▬▬▬▬▬▬ *11.59

CLASS 2P 4-4-0

No	Allocation
40582	▬▬▬ 1.50 BANK HALL
40584	▬▬▬ 8.50 BANK HALL
40588	▬▬▬ 1.50 LOWER DARWEN
40676	ACCRINGTON 5.51 ▬ 7.51 NUNEATON
40680	ACCRINGTON 9.52 ▬▬▬ 7.53 WIGAN (L&Y)
40682	BACUP 10.50 ▬▬▬ 7.52 FARNLEY JUNCTION 9.52 ▬▬▬ 7.53 BOLTON
40691	BACUP 10.50 ▬▬▬ 7.52 FARNLEY JUNCTION

CLASS 4P 2-6-4T

PAGE	No	Allocation
	42054	AINTREE 3.64 ▬ *7.64
	42063	CHESTER 9.56 ▬▬▬▬▬ 6.59 SOUTHPORT
7·8	42079	LEES (OLDHAM) 4.64 ▬▬▬ 8.66 TRAFFORD PARK
	42087	BOLTON 6.64 ▬▬ 7.66 BIRKENHEAD
7	42115	LEES (OLDHAM) 4.64 ▬▬▬ 8.66 BARROW
	42278	▬▬▬▬▬ 4.57 HELLIFIELD
8·9	42279	▬▬▬▬▬▬▬ 9.58 NEASDEN
151	42280	▬▬▬▬▬▬ 7.58 LANCASTER ROSE GROVE 1.60 ▬▬▬ *3.64
	42281	▬▬▬▬▬ 7.57 LANCASTER
	42282	▬▬▬▬▬ 5.58 NEASDEN
	42283	▬▬▬▬▬ 5.58 NEASDEN CHESTER 8.65 ▬▬ 8.66 TRAFFORD PARK
10	42284	▬▬▬▬▬ 5.58 NEASDEN
	42285	▬▬▬▬ 3.56 MIRFIELD
	42286	▬▬▬▬▬ 6.58 BANK HALL
9	42287	▬▬▬▬▬▬ 10.59 AGECROFT
	42288	▬▬▬▬▬▬▬ *10.63
	42289	▬▬▬▬ 7.56 BOLTON
	42290	▬▬▬▬ 7.57 SOUTHPORT
	42379	BUXTON 7.63 ▬ *8.64
	42450	CHESTER 9.56 ▬▬ 8.58 NEASDEN
	42451	CHESTER 9.56 ▬▬ 7.58 LANCASTER 8.58 ▬▬ 6.59 SOUTHPORT
	42461	CHESTER 9.56 ▬▬ 8.58 LANCASTER
	42464	LANCASTER 3.64 ▬▬ *8.65
	42477	▬▬▬ 9.50 GOOLE
	42485	LOWER DARWEN 4.61 ▬ 6.61 SOUTHPORT
11	42486	▬▬▬▬▬ 7.58 ROWSLEY
	42492	LOSTOCK HALL 10.63 ▬▬ *6.65
	42542	STOKE 6.65 ▬ *7.65
	42548	ACCRINGTON 3.59 ▬▬▬▬▬▬ 8.66 BIRKENHEAD
13	42549	ACCRINGTON 3.59 ▬▬▬ *11.61
	42550	▬▬▬▬▬ 3.57 BOLTON
	42551	▬▬▬ 8.51 ACCRINGTON
	42568	CHESTER 9.56 ▬▬ 8.58 NEASDEN 8.59 ▬▬ 9.59 NEASDEN
11	42614	TRAFFORD PARK 9.62 ▬▬ *5.64
	42618	▬▬▬▬▬ 4.57 BOLTON 5.58 ▬▬ 8.58 NEASDEN

CLASS 4P 2-6-4T contd.

PAGE	No	Allocations
	42619	ACCRINGTON 1.60 — *6.64
155	**42620**	ACCRINGTON 1.60 — *9.64
12	**42621**	— 6.58 SOUTHPORT
13	**42622**	— 5.56 LOW MOOR
12·14	**42623**	— *2.64
14	**42624**	— 4.60 WIGAN (L&Y)
	42625	— 5.54 BURY
	42626	— 9.52 BOLTON
	42630	— 9.52 BOLTON
	42632	WIGAN (L&Y) 9.62 — *6.63
	42635	— 9.52 BOLTON
	42640	WIGAN (L&Y) 9.62 — *9.64
	42651	BURY 9.54 — 11.59 LANDORE 4.60 — *9.64
	42656	BOLTON 6.64 — 8.66 BOLTON
13·14	**42660**	CHESTER 9.56 — 1.61 PATRICROFT 6.64 — 1.65 LOSTOCK HALL
	42676	BOLTON 9.65 — *6.66
	42686	BEDFORD 7.63 — *5.64
8·10	**42696**	MOTHERWELL 2.60 — *9.64
	42697	ARDROSSAN 2.60 — 4.60 WIGAN (L&Y) 4.60 — 5.64 BARROW
	42698	GREENOCK 2.60 — *10.63

Fowler Class 4P 2-6-4T No **42379**

Stanier Class 4P 2-6-4T No **42624**

Hughes/Fowler Class 5MT 2-6-0 No **42726**

CLASS 5MT 2-6-0

PAGE	No	Allocations
	42700**	— 8.50 MIRFIELD; GORTON 6.65 — 11.65 BIRKENHEAD
	42701	— 7.63 GORTON
24	**42702**	— 10.56 FARNLEY JUNCTION
	42703	— 11.60 ROSE GROVE
22	**42704**	— 9.62 BOLTON
23	**42705**	— 9.62 BOLTON
	42706	— 8.50 ROSE GROVE
15·18·152	**42707**	— 1.60 FLEETWOOD
20	**42708**	— 2.53 THORNTON JUNCTION 3.53 — 9.62 BOLTON
	42709	— 5.63 BOLTON
16·18·21	**42710**	— 7.63 GORTON
	42711	— 3.57 AINTREE
	42713	— 5.56 FARNLEY JUNCTION
17·19·23	**42714**	— *10.62
16·18·20	**42715**	AGECROFT 1.50 — 1.60 BOLTON GORTON 6.65 — 10.65 STOCKPORT EDGELEY
20	**42726**	AINTREE 5.54 — *10.62
	42727	AINTREE 5.54 — 3.57 AINTREE
	42728	AINTREE 5.54 — 11.60 ROSE GROVE
	42732	AINTREE 5.54 — 2.57 FLEETWOOD
19·22	**42733**	AINTREE 5.54 — 7.63 GORTON
15·17·21	**42750**	— 7.63 GORTON
	42766	— 5.56 FARNLEY JUNCTION
	42785	CREWE SOUTH 7.59 — 9.59 CREWE SOUTH
	42787	CREWE SOUTH 7.58 — 9.58 CREWE SOUTH
	42789	— 5.56 FARNLEY JUNCTION
	42820	— 11.54 BURY
	42831	GORTON 6.65 — 10.65 BIRKENHEAD
	42844	LOWER DARWEN 8.65 — *8.65
	42845	ROWSLEY 1.50 — 2.52 HUDDERSFIELD
	42852	WILLESDEN 6.59 — 9.59 WILLESDEN
	42853	BESCOT 7.58 — 9.58 BESCOT
	42871	— 2.53 THORNTON JUNCTION 3.53 — 7.63 GORTON
16	**42878**	KINGMOOR 1.50 — 2.53 THORNTON JUNCTION 3.53 — 3.57 AINTREE
	42901	— 11.53 ST. MARGARETS (EDINBURGH) 4.54 — 11.60 ROSE GROVE
	42905	GORTON 6.65 — *7.65
	42938	GORTON 6.65 — *9.65
24	**42963**	CREWE NORTH 6.59 — 9.59 CREWE NORTH
	42970	BIRKENHEAD 6.59 — 9.59 BIRKENHEAD

CLASS 4F 0-6-0 (Midland)

	43756	BELLE VUE 4.56 ▬▬▬ 5.57 HELLIFIELD
	43947	KETTERING 10.63 ▬ 8.64 BUXTON
28	43952	WIGAN (L&Y) 9.62 ▬ 12.63 LOWER DARWEN
	43979	SALTLEY 4.64 ▬ *11.64
25·27·29	44022	BELLE VUE 4.56 ▬▬▬▬▬ *11.63

CLASS 4F 0-6-0 (LMS)

	44040	BELLE VUE 9.55 ▪ 11.55 WALTON-ON-THE-HILL
	44092	SALTLEY 4.64 ▬ *9.64
	44119	BELLE VUE 3.56 ▬ 9.57 SKIPTON
30	44221	WIGAN (L&Y) 9.62 ▬ *5.64
	44247	BUXTON 10.64 ▬ *12.65
25·26·30	44311	▬▬▬▬▬▬ 6.61 BURY
26·28	44431	HELLIFIELD 8.60 ▬▬ *9.64
	44460	LOWER DARWEN 11.63 ▬ *10.64
	44481	WALTON-ON-THE-HILL 12.63 ▬ *11.64
	44486	BELLE VUE 4.56 ▪ 11.56 WIGAN (L&Y)
26·27·30	44543	▬▬▬▬▬▬ *5.64
	44544	GORTON 11.64 ▬ *4.65

CLASS 5MT 4-6-0

	44676	AINTREE 6.63 ▬ *7.64
33·45	44696	▬▬▬▬ 2.64 TRAFFORD PARK STOCKPORT 6.65 ▬ *5.67
34·45·50	44697	▪ 1.51 BANK HALL ACCRINGTON 8.51 ▪ 2.52 BANK HALL 5.52 ▪ 1.53 BLACKPOOL MILLHOUSES 5.53 ▪ 7.53 FARNLEY JCTN 8.53 ▬ *11.67
34·45·47	44734	▬▬▬▬▬▬ *12.67
42·53	44735	▬▬▬▬▬ 11.64 TRAFFORD PARK 3.68 ▬ 7.68 CARNFORTH
35·47·49·52	44736	▬▬▬▬▬ 1.64 PATRICROFT BOLTON 4.66 ▬ *9.67
	44746	LONGSIGHT 4.60 ▬ 9.60 AGECROFT
	44778	BLACKPOOL 4.51 ▪ 5.51 BLACKPOOL
	44780	SPRINGS BRANCH 12.67 ▬ *7.68
	44781	TRAFFORD PARK 10.67 ▬ *5.68
	44782	▬▬▬ 8.50 AGECROFT
43·44·46	44803	BELLE VUE 4.56 ▬▬▬ *7.68
	44809	WARRINGTON 10.67 ▬ 7.68 CARNFORTH
	44817	BOLTON 6.63 ▬ 11.63 AGECROFT
51	44818	BOLTON 6.63 ▬ *7.68
	44822	BOLTON 6.63 ▬ 11.63 AGECROFT 6.65 ▬ *10.67
34·51	44845	BELLE VUE 4.56 ▬▬▬ *7.68
	44846	ANNESLEY 7.65 ▬ *1.68
	44851	TRAFFORD PARK 3.68 ▬ *4.68
	44861	DERBY 7.65 ▬ *11.67
	44884	KINGMOOR 1.68 ▬ *7.68
	44888	▬▬▬ 12.50 SALTLEY
	44889	▬▬▬▬ 8.52 ACCRINGTON
31·54	44890	▬▬▬▬▬▬ *7.68
36·39·153	44891	▬▬▬▬▬▬ *7.68
	44892	▬▬▬ 8.50 PRESTON CARNFORTH 7.58 ▪ 9.58 CARNFORTH
36·44	44893	▬▬▬▬ 11.56 BANK HALL 12.56 ▬▬▬ 1.64 PATRICROFT BOLTON 4.66 ▬ *11.67
	44894	▬▬▬▬ 11.58 BANK HALL 2.59 ▬ 2.60 ROSE GROVE
	44895	▬▬▬▬▬ 11.64 TRAFFORD PARK
	44910	KINGMOOR 1.68 ▬ *7.68
36·45·50	44933	▬▬▬▬▬▬ 1.66 LANCASTER
48·50	44934	▬▬▬▬▬▬ 8.66 WARRINGTON
	44938	BLETCHLEY 7.65 ▬▬ *12.67
	44940	▬▬▬ 11.53 ROSE GROVE
	44949	PATRICROFT 6.65 ▬▬▬ *7.68
	44951	▬▬▬ 8.50 LOW MOOR
	44962	SPRINGS BRANCH 12.67 ▬ *12.67
	44987	▬▬▬ 2.53 WAKEFIELD
	45017	SOUTHPORT 6.64 ▬ 11.64 TRAFFORD PARK
	45026	PATRICROFT 6.65 ▬ *10.65
39	45031	BELLE VUE 4.56 ▬▬▬ 1.60 MOLD JUNCTION
	45057	SPRINGS BRANCH 7.63 ▬ 10.63 SPEKE JUNCTION
	45068	BANK HALL 1.51 ▪ 2.51 BANK HALL
	45073	SPRINGS BRANCH 7.63 ▬ 11.64 TRAFFORD PARK
	45076	FARNLEY JUNCTION 8.56 ▬▬▬▬ *7.68
	45077	PATRICROFT 6.65 ▬ *8.65
	45079	▬▬▬ 11.52 HUDDERSFIELD
	45083	SOUTHPORT 6.64 ▬▬ *12.67
41·43	45101	WAKEFIELD 8.56 ▬▬▬▬ *3.63
151	45102	▬▬▬▬▬ 7.60 BLACKPOOL
	45103	▬▬▬▬ 7.60 PATRICROFT KINGMOOR 7.63 ▬ 10.63 SPEKE JUNCTION
38·42	45104	AGECROFT 6.50 ▬▬▬▬ 1.64 AINTREE 6.64 ▬ 11.64 BURY
35	45105	▬▬▬▬▬ 1.61 SOUTHPORT
	45109	SPRINGS BRANCH 7.63 ▪ 8.63 SOUTHPORT
46	45118	AINTREE 6.63 ▬ 10.63 KINGMOOR

159

CLASS 5MT 4-6-0 contd.

	45133	AGECROFT 6.65 ▬ 8.66 WARRINGTON
	45150	WARRINGTON 6.64 ▬ 11.64 TRAFFORD PARK
37·46	**45154***	ST. ROLLOX 3.57 ▬▬▬▬ 1.64 AINTREE 6.64 ▬ 7.64 CARNFORTH
32	**45156***	ST. ROLLOX 3.57 ▬▬▬▬ 12.62 BOLTON
	45195	KINGMOOR 7.63 ▬ 10.63 KINGMOOR
	45200	STOCKPORT (EDGELEY) 5.68 ▬ 7.68 CARNFORTH
151·156	**45202**	▬▬▬▬▬▬▬▬▬▬▬▬▬ *7.68
	45203	▬▬▬▬▬▬▬▬▬▬▬▬▬ *7.68
	45205	ROSE GROVE 2.66 ▬ *10.66
	45206	FLEETWOOD 7.65 ▬▬▬ 7.68 CARNFORTH
	45210	LOW MOOR 5.50 ▬ 10.50 HUDDERSFIELD
	45211	LOW MOOR 10.50 ▬ 12.50 FARNLEY JUNCTION
	45216	BANK HALL 2.51 ▬ 4.51 BANK HALL
	45219	AGECROFT 4.48 ▬ 10.50 HUDDERSFIELD
151·156	**45220**	AGECROFT 6.50 ▬▬▬▬▬▬▬▬▬ 2.64 TRAFFORD PARK
	45222	▬▬▬▬ 12.50 HUDDERSFIELD COLWICK 11.66 ▬ *7.68
42	**45223**	AGECROFT 4.48 ▬▬▬▬ 5.53 NINE ELMS 6.53 ▬▬ 2.57 AGECROFT
152	**45224**	▬▬▬▬▬▬▬▬▬▬▬▬ 12.62 BOLTON
31	**45225**	SHEFFIELD 10.50 ▬▬▬▬▬▬▬ 1.60 MOLD JUNCTION
38·44·53	**45232**	▬▬▬▬▬▬▬▬▬▬▬ 12.62 BOLTON
37·44	**45233**	▬▬▬▬▬▬▬▬▬▬▬▬▬ 11.64 TRAFFORD PARK
	45234	▬▬▬▬▬▬ 12.56 AGECROFT ROSE GROVE 2.66 ▬ *9.67
33·38	**45246**	UPPERBY 7.63 ▬▬▬▬▬ *12.67
	45252	PATRICROFT 8.64 ▬▬ 12.64 BURY
	45254	KINGMOOR 1.68 ▬ *5.68
	45255	PATRICROFT 1.61 ▬▬▬▬▬▬ *7.68
	45268	SPRINGS BRANCH 12.67 ▬▬ 7.68 CARNFORTH
52	**45271**	WARRINGTON 6.64 ▬▬▬▬ *9.67
	45284	BELLE VUE 8.54 ▬▬▬ 1.60 WILLESDEN
	45290	BEDFORD 2.57 ▬▬▬ 2.62 BOLTON
	45291	STOCKPORT (EDGELEY) 6.65 ▬ *11.65
	45310	SPRINGS BRANCH 12.67 ▬▬ 7.68 CARNFORTH
	45330	WARRINGTON 10.67 ▬▬ 7.68 CARNFORTH
155	**45336**	BANK HALL 10.50 ▬▬▬▬▬▬▬▬▬▬▬ *1.67
	45339	LONGSIGHT 4.60 ▬▬▬▬▬▬▬ 8.66 ROSE GROVE
	45341	FARNLEY JUNCTION 8.56 ▬▬▬▬▬▬▬▬ *1.67
	45343	WARRINGTON 6.64 ▬▬▬ 8.66 ROSE GROVE
	45368	UPPERBY 6.63 ▬ 11.63 AGECROFT
	45380	SPRINGS BRANCH 7.63 ▬ 8.63 LONGSIGHT
	45381	WARRINGTON 6.64 ▬▬ 11.64 BURY
48	**45382**	STOCKPORT (EDGELEY) 6.65 ▬▬ 8.66 ROSE GROVE
	45388	SPRINGS BRANCH 7.63 ▬ 10.63 SPEKE JUNCTION
	45409	PATRICROFT 8.64 ▬ 9.64 BOLTON
	45411	BOLTON 4.66 ▬▬ *7.68
	45420	AGECROFT 6.65 ▬▬ *7.68
33·48	**45435**	WAKEFIELD 8.56 ▬▬▬▬▬▬▬▬▬ 1.66 LANCASTER
	45437	UPPERBY 6.63 ▬ 11.63 AGECROFT
	45451	AINTREE 6.64 ▬ 7.64 CARNFORTH

Fowler Class 4F 0-6-0 No **44543**

Stanier Class 5 4-6-0 No **45233**

Fowler Patriot Class 6P 4-6-0 No **45539**
E.C. Trench

PATRIOT CLASS 4-6-0

55 - 62	**45500***	CARNFORTH 3.60 ▬▬ *3.61
55·57·59	**45503***	CREWE NORTH 7.58 ▬ 9.58 CREWE NORTH
61	**45509***	DERBY 8.58 ▬▬▬ *8.61
57·58·60	**45515***	EDGE HILL 4.60 ▬▬▬ *6.62
56·62	**45522***	KENTISH TOWN 9.61 ▬▬▬ 6.63 LONGSIGHT
58·62	**45539***	CARNFORTH 3.60 ▬▬▬ *9.61

JUBILEE CLASS 4-6-0

	45558*	PATRICROFT 8.64 ▬ *9.64
	45564*	LEEDS HOLBECK 7.64 ▬ *8.64
	45568*	LEEDS HOLBECK 4.64 ▬ *5.64
90	**45578***	ASTON 1.62 ▬▬ *6.64

Stanier Jubilee Class 6P 4-6-0 No **45642**
Boscawen

Royal Scot Class 7P 4-6-0 No **46133**
The Green Howards

Ivatt Class 2MT 2-6-0 No **46437**

PAGE   1948 ──➤ 1968

JUBILEE CLASS 4-6-0 contd.

	45580*	WARRINGTON 9.64 ▬ *12.64
79	**45585***	LEICESTER 6.61 ▬ 9.61 LEICESTER
	45590*	AGECROFT 6.63 ▬ 9.63 WARRINGTON
79	**45592***	CARNFORTH 6.64 ▬ *9.64
	45593**	PATRICROFT 1.65 ▬ 4.65 LEEDS HOLBECK
66·67	**45600***	PATRICROFT 1.65 ▬▬ *12.65
69	**45601***	WILLESDEN 6.60 ▬▬▬▬ *9.64
70	**45602***	MILLHOUSES 3.62 ▬▬ 9.64 WAKEFIELD
70	**45604***	WARRINGTON 4.65 ▬ *7.65
	45614*	KENTISH TOWN 7.59 ▬ 9.59 KENTISH TOWN
	45615*	LEICESTER 7.61 ▬ 9.61 LEICESTER
	45622*	KENTISH TOWN 7.61 ▌7.61 KENTISH TOWN
83·84	**45623***	CREWE SOUTH 3.62 ▬▬ *8.64
87	**45628***	KENTISH TOWN 7.61 ▬ 9.61 KENTISH TOWN
	45632*	STOCKPORT EDGELEY 8.65 ▬ *10.65
88·89·152/4	**45635***	▬▬▬▬▬▬▬▬▬▬▬▬▬▬▬ 2.64 KINGMOOR
	45636*	LEICESTER 6.61 ▬ 9.61 LEICESTER
67·68·154	**45642***	▬▬▬▬▬▬▬▬▬▬▬▬▬▬▬▬ *1.65
	45650*	LEICESTER 6.61 ▌8.61 LEICESTER
77	**45652***	LEICESTER 6.60 ▬▬▬ 7.63 WARRINGTON
	45653*	BLACKPOOL 6.64 ▬▬ *4.65
78·94	**45654***	AGECROFT 6.63 ▬ 3.64 STOCKPORT EDGELEY 10.65 ▬ *6.66
91·92	**45661***	▬▬▬▬▬▬▬▬▬▬▬▬ 8.64 LEEDS HOLBECK
82	**45664***	AGECROFT 6.63 ▬ 9.63 WARRINGTON
85	**45671***	FARNLEY JUNCTION 9.48 ▬▬▬▬▬ 10.57 LONGSIGHT
65	**45679***	LONGSIGHT 6.60 ▬▬▬ *12.62
	45698*	SOUTHPORT 9.48 ▌11.48 BANK HALL
63·64·153	**45700***	▬▬▬▬▬▬▬▬▬ 8.57 BLACKPOOL 9.57 ▬▬▬▬▬ 3.63 DERBY
72·73	**45701***	▬▬▬▬▬▬▬▬▬▬▬ *2.63
71·155	**45702***	FARNLEY JUNCTION 12.50 ▬▬▬▬▬ *5.63
85·86	**45705***	BLACKPOOL 6.64 ▬▬ *11.65
74·75	**45706***	▬▬▬▬▬▬▬▬▬▬▬ *9.63
80·81·82	**45710***	▌9.48 BANK HALL 9.48 ▬▬▬▬▬▬ *6.64
74	**45711***	▌9.48 FARNLEY JUNCTION
93	**45712***	▬▬▬▬▬▬ 2.57 TRAFFORD PARK KENTISH TOWN 6.61 ▬ 9.61 KENTISH TOWN
87·154	**45716***	AGECROFT 6.63 ▬ 7.64 LEEDS HOLBECK
	45717*	▌4.48 SOUTHPORT
76	**45719***	▬▬▬▬▬▬▬▬ 4.53 BANK HALL
65	**45737***	CREWE NORTH 2.62 ▬▬▬ *6.64

ROYAL SCOT CLASS 4-6-0

96	**46106***	LONGSIGHT 4.60 ▬▬▬ 12.60 TRAFFORD PARK
	46133*	KENTISH TOWN 9.61 ▬▬ *2.63
	46137*	LONGSIGHT 4.60 ▬▬▬ 12.60 TRAFFORD PARK
95	**46139***	KENTISH TOWN 9.61 ▬▬ *10.62
95·96·97·98	**46140***	KENTISH TOWN 9.61 ▬▬▬ 6.63 LONGSIGHT
96·97·98	**46142***	KENTISH TOWN 9.61 ▬▬▬ 6.63 LONGSIGHT

CLASS 2 2-6-0

102	**46406**	BURY 4.65 ▬▬▬ *1.67
	46410	BLACKPOOL 11.53 ▬▬▬▬▬ 7.57 LANCASTER
104	**46411**	BLACKPOOL 11.53 ▬▬▬▬▬▬▬▬▬▬▬▬▬▬▬ *1.67
102	**46412**	BURY 4.65 ▬▬▬ *8.66
	46417	BOLTON 9.66 ▬▬▬ *2.67
100·103	**46418**	▬▬▬▬▬▬▬▬▬▬▬▬▬▬▬▬▬▬▬▬ *1.67
	46419	▬▬▬▬▬▬▬▬▬▬▬ 9.62 LEES (OLDHAM)
	46436	BOLTON 8.66 ▬▬▬ *5.67
103·104	**46437**	GOOLE 3.56 ▬▬▬▬▬▬▬▬▬▬▬ *5.67
	46443**	SALTLEY 10.66 ▬▬ *3.67
	46448	SALTLEY 10.66 ▬▬▬ *5.67
	46449	LEES (OLDHAM) 4.64 ▬▬▬▬ *5.67
100·101	**46452**	LEES (OLDHAM) 4.64 ▬▬▬ 9.65 WORKINGTON

CLASS 2 2-6-0 contd.

	46472	NORTHWICH 8.64 *1.65
99	46484	NEW 10.51 6.62 LEES (OLDHAM)
99·100	46485	NEW 10.51 11.53 AGECROFT — LEES (OLDHAM) 4.64 7.65 WORKINGTON
	46486	NEW 10.51 1.52 BLACKPOOL
101·155	46487	NEW 11.51 9.63 LEES (OLDHAM)
101	46490	SALTLEY 8.66 *5.67
	46501	BURY 4.65 *5.67
	46504	BOLTON 8.66 *10.66
104	46505	SALTLEY 8.66 5.67 BUXTON
	46506	BOLTON 8.66 *5.67
	46513	OSWESTRY 1.65 6.65 CARLISLE UPPERBY
	46514	OSWESTRY 1.65 6.65 LANCASTER
	46523	MACHYNLLETH 8.63 6.65 AINTREE

MIDLAND 'JINTY' 0-6-0T

105·106·107	47202	AGECROFT 8.66 *12.66
106	47207	CRICKLEWOOD 1.58 *2.64
	47208	WELLINGBOROUGH 1.58 *1.59
	47217	CRICKLEWOOD 11.58 *8.62
	47230	AGECROFT 8.63 10.63 EDGE HILL

'JINTY' 0-6-0T

	47284	PATRICROFT 4.60 *9.64
	47300	PATRICROFT 9.62 *8.63
	47301	BROMSGROVE 12.56 2.57 BANK HALL
	47303	BROMSGROVE 12.56 2.57 BANK HALL
	47305	BROMSGROVE 12.56 2.57 AINTREE
105	47362	CARNFORTH 8.65 *11.65
106·107·108	47383**	ROSE GROVE 1.66 12.66 WESTHOUSES
108	47388	BOLTON 7.63 *12.66
	47408	CARLISLE UPPERBY 6.63 *11.65
	47425	BROMSGROVE 12.56 2.57 AINTREE
	47440	BELLE VUE 4.56 *12.59
108	47480	AINTREE 3.64 *9.65
	47493**	SPEKE JUNCTION 12.58 4.59 SPEKE JUNCTION
	47517	BARROW 12.58 4.59 BARROW
	47546	CANKLOW 2.59 *7.62
107	47547	CANKLOW 2.59 *12.63
	47576	ROSE GROVE 8.60 *9.60
	47577	8.54 ROSE GROVE
	47582	LOW MOOR 12.60 *8.63
	47586	8.54 ROSE GROVE
	47631	ROSE GROVE 1.66 *6.66
	47640	ARDSLEY 12.60 *9.64
	47656	WIDNES 11.63 *12.65
	47660	ROSE GROVE 3.64 *12.65
	47681	AGECROFT 6.65 *8.65

CLASS 8F 2-8-0

	48010	SPEKE JUNCTION 4.66 *1.68
	48026	AGECROFT 6.66 2.68 BOLTON
	48036	
114	48046	WESTHOUSES 3.66 1.68 BOLTON
112	48090	CHESTER 3.67 2.68 BOLTON
109	48106	WARRINGTON DALLAM 11.63 10.64 BURY
	48110	WILLESDEN 10.50 11.50 SHREWSBURY
	48115	TOTON 10.58 1.63 PATRICROFT
	48120	STAVELEY BARROW HILL 1.50 6.50 BESCOT
	48132	SPRINGS BRANCH 12.67 *6.68
	48136	CARLISLE KINGMOOR 7.64 *3.67
110	48148	HEATON MERSEY 10.58 1.63 PATRICROFT
	48171	STOKE 8.65 11.65 BUXTON
	48173**	WILLESDEN 10.48 11.49 RUGBY
	48174	STAFFORD 7.65 *5.67
	48197	COLWICK 9.66 3.68 HEATON MERSEY
	48200	EDGE HILL 8.66 1.68 BOLTON
111·113	48318	12.49 8.50 BESCOT — CARLISLE KINGMOOR 6.64 10.64 AGECROFT 11.64 *10.66
113	48321	CARLISLE KINGMOOR 6.64 *7.68
	48331	STAVELEY BARROW HILL 4.64 *2.66
	48335	STOCKPORT EDGELEY 10.67 1.68 ROSE GROVE
	48345	STOCKPORT EDGELEY 10.67 1.68 TRAFFORD PARK
	48356	HEATON MERSEY 5.68 *7.68
	48368	STOKE 8.67 *7.68
	48369	SHREWSBURY 8.65 1.66 BUXTON 11.67 *7.68
	48372	BIRKENHEAD 10.58 6.63 CARLISLE KINGMOOR 6.64 *12.66
	48373	STOCKPORT EDGELEY 10.67 *7.68

Midland Class 3F 0-6-0T No **47202**

LMS Class 3F 0-6-0T No **47388**

Stanier Class 8F 2-8-0 No **48557**

CLASS 8F 2-8-0 contd.

	48389	SALTLEY 3.48 ▮▮ 8.49 LONGSIGHT	
	48391		STAVELEY BARROW HILL 4.64 ▮▮▮▮▮ *12.65
	48397		CARLISLE KINGMOOR 6.64 ▮▮ 10.64 AGECROFT
	48426		CARLISLE KINGMOOR 7.64 ▮▮▮▮ *6.66
	48464		CARLISLE KINGMOOR 7.64 ▮▮ 12.64 STOCKPORT EDGELEY
	48471		SHREWSBURY 5.66 ▮▮▮ 11.67 BUXTON
	48491		WARRINGTON 10.58 ▮▮▮▮▮ 1.63 PATRICROFT
	48515		STAVELEY BARROW HILL 5.63 ▮▮▮ 12.63 WARRINGTON
	48518**	BESCOT 11.50 ▮ 12.50 WILLESDEN	
	48523		PATRICROFT 11.63 ▮▮▮▮ 10.64 BURY
114	48529		EDGE HILL 5.68 ▮ *7.68
	48532		PATRICROFT 8.64 ▮▮ 10.65 BUXTON
110	48533		STAVELEY BARROW HILL 4.64 ▮▮▮▮▮▮ *5.68
	48536		AGECROFT 4.66 ▮▮ 8.66 EDGE HILL
	48539		STAVELEY BARROW HILL 12.63 ▮▮▮▮ 11.64 AGECROFT
	48543		GORTON 6.65 ▮▮▮ *2.66
110	48553		WELLINGBOROUGH 10.58 ▮▮▮▮▮ 12.63 PATRICROFT
112	48557		GORTON 6.65 ▮▮▮ *7.67
	48602		STAFFORD 7.65 ▮▮▮ *7.67
112	48612		CARLISLE KINGMOOR 6.64 ▮ 3.66 HEATON MERSEY 12.66 ▮▮ *7.68
	48618		STAVELEY BARROW HILL 5.63 ▮▮▮ 2.64 FLEETWOOD
	48620		COLWICK 11.66 ▮▮▮▮▮▮ *7.68
	48655		CHESTER 3.67 ▮▮ *8.67
	48665		EDGE HILL 5.68 ▮ 7.68 ROSE GROVE
	48678		SPRINGS BRANCH 12.67 ▮▮ *7.68
	48686	STAVELEY BARROW HILL 1.50 ▮▮ 6.50 BESCOT	
	48687		EDGE HILL 5.68 ▮ *7.68
	48691		HEATON MERSEY 2.66 ▮*3.66
109	48705	ACCRINGTON 8.49 ▮▮ 8.51 BESCOT	
	48706	NORTHWICH 11.50 ▮12.50 SWANSEA VICTORIA	
	48707	AINTREE 8.49 ▮▮▮ 1.51 SHREWSBURY	
	48708		CARLISLE KINGMOOR 9.64 ▮ 10.64 AGECROFT
	48713	AINTREE 2.51 ▮▮ 8.51 BESCOT	
	48714	ROSE GROVE 1.50 ▮▮ 10.50 BELLE VUE	
	48715	ROSE GROVE 1.50 ▮▮ 10.50 BELLE VUE	
	48716		NUNEATON 10.58 ▮▮▮▮▮ 1.63 PATRICROFT
	48718	NORTHWICH 11.50 ▮▮ 1.51 BIRKENHEAD	
	48719	LOSTOCK HALL 1.50 ▮▮ 12.50 BIRKENHEAD	
	48720	9.50 ▮▮ 1.51 BIRKENHEAD	WARRINGTON 10.58 ▮▮▮▮▮ 1.63 PATRICROFT
	48722	WAKEFIELD 8.50 ▮▮ 8.51 BESCOT	
	48725	AGECROFT 12.50 ▮▮ 8.51 BESCOT	
	48726	WAKEFIELD 1.50 ▮▮ 12.50 BIRKENHEAD	
	48727	WAKEFIELD 8.50 ▮▮ 8.51 BESCOT	
	48730	WAKEFIELD 1.50 ▮▮ 11.50 SHREWSBURY	
	48733	HUDDERSFIELD 3.48 ▮▮ 8.51 BESCOT	
	48735	FARNLEY JUNCTION 3.50 ▮ 12.50 SWANSEA VICTORIA	
	48737	BUXTON 11.50 ▮ 11.50 SWANSEA VICTORIA	
	48739	FARNLEY JUNCTION 3.50 ▮▮ 12.51 SHREWSBURY	
	48742		EDGE HILL 8.66 ▮▮ *8.67
	48744		STOCKPORT EDGELEY 6.65 ▮ 1.66 BUXTON
114	48745		LONGSIGHT 11.58 ▮▮▮▮▮ 1.63 PATRICROFT
	48746		EDGE HILL 5.68 ▮ *7.68
	48751	MIRFIELD 9.50 ▮▮ 12.50 CREWE SOUTH	
	48752	MIRFIELD 1.50 ▮▮ 8.51 BESCOT	
	48754	FARNLEY JUNCTION 3.50 ▮▮ 12.50 CREWE SOUTH	
	48755	MIRFIELD 9.50 ▮▮ 8.51 BESCOT	
	48756	NORTHWICH 11.50 ▮12.50 CREWE SOUTH	CARLISLE KINGMOOR 7.64 ▮▮▮▮ *1.67
111	48758		CARLISLE KINGMOOR 6.64 ▮▮▮▮ *12.67
	48760	▮▮▮▮▮ 8.50 AGECROFT	
	48761	▮▮▮▮▮ 11.50 SWANSEA VICTORIA	
	48762	▮▮▮▮▮ 8.50 BOLTON	
	48763	▮▮▮▮▮ 8.50 SALTLEY	
	48765		STAVELEY BARROW HILL 4.64 ▮▮▮▮ 11.65 STOCKPORT EDGELEY
	48766	AGECROFT 12.50 ▮▮ 8.51 BESCOT	
	48768	GOOLE 9.50 ▮ 11.50 SWANSEA VICTORIA	
	48769	BURY 3.49 ▮▮▮ 8.51 BESCOT	
	48775		CARLISLE KINGMOOR 6.64 ▮▮▮▮ 6.66 AGECROFT

LMS CLASS 7F 0-8-0

116-119·156	**49508**	BURY 3.53 ▬▬▬▬▬▬▬ 11.60 AGECROFT
	49510	▬▬ 8.49 BOLTON
	49511	AINTREE 11.55 ▬▬▬▬ *5.59
	49512	▬▬*5.49
115	**49515**	AINTREE 11.55 ▬▬▬▬▬ *11.59
	49516	WAKEFIELD 10.49 ▪*12.49
	49520	▬▬ *5.50
	49529	WAKEFIELD 10.49 ▪*12.49
	49531	WAKEFIELD 10.49 ▬▬*10.50
	49533	▬▬▬▬*12.49
	49536	AINTREE 6.50 ▬▬ 5.51 LEES (OLDHAM)
	49541	WAKEFIELD 9.49 ▪*10.49
	49544	BOLTON 1.60 ▪*2.60
	49545	WAKEFIELD 9.49 ▬▬ 11.50 AINTREE
	49546	WAKEFIELD 3.48 ▬▬*8.49
	49552	SOWERBY BRIDGE 6.56 ▪*8.56
	49554	▬▬▬▬▬ 11.50 AINTREE
	49556	WAKEFIELD 3.48 ▬▬*8.49
	49557	BURY 12.51 ▬▬▬▬*11.55
	49558	WAKEFIELD 10.49 ▬▬▬*4.51
	49559	WAKEFIELD 3.48 ▬▬*3.49
118	**49560**	▬▬▬▬▬▬▬*12.57
115·117	**49565**	▬▬▬▬ *4.49
	49570	AGECROFT 12.50 ▬▬▬▬*9.55
	49574	WAKEFIELD 9.49 ▬▬*8.50
	49580	HUDDERSFIELD 6.50 ▬▬ *3.51
	49583	HUDDERSFIELD 6.50 ▬▬*9.50
	49591	BURY 12.51 ▬▬ *12.52
	49592	SOWERBY BRIDGE 12.57 ▬▬▬*5.59
	49607	▬▬*8.49
	49608	▬▬▬▬▬ 5.51 LEES (OLDHAM)
	49611	LOSTOCK HALL 3.48 ▪*8.49
	49612	LOSTOCK HALL 3.48 ▬▬▬ 10.50 WIGAN (L&Y)
119	**49618**	BOLTON 1.60 ▬▬ 7.61 AGECROFT
116·117	**49624**	SOWERBY BRIDGE 6.56 ▬▬▬▬*2.60
	49625	WAKEFIELD 9.49 ▬▬ 10.50 WIGAN (L&Y)
	49636	▬▬▬▬*9.50
	49637	▬▬▬▬▬ 2.51 WIGAN (L&Y)
	49639	▬▬*8.49
	49642	▬▬*8.49
	49650	▬▬▬▬▬ 11.50 SOWERBY BRIDGE
	49651	▬▬▬▬▬*12.50
	49652	▬▬*8.49
	49653	▬▬▬▬*8.50
	49654	▬▬▬*12.49
	49655	▬▬▬*4.50
	49656	▬▬*8.49
	49657	▬▬▬▬▬ 11.50 SOWERBY BRIDGE
	49660	MIRFIELD 10.50 ▪11.50 SOWERBY BRIDGE
118	**49661**	MIRFIELD 10.50 ▪11.50 SOWERBY BRIDGE
120	**49666**	BURY 11.53 ▬▬▬*5.56
	49667	BURY 11.53 ▬▬▬▬*5.59
	49670	WAKEFIELD 5.48 ▬▬ *8.49
	49673	FARNLEY JUNCTION 3.48 ▬▬▬ 11.50 SOWERBY BRIDGE
	49674	BANK HALL 3.48 ▬▬▬▬ 11.50 SOWERBY BRIDGE

CLASS 2P 2-4-2T

50736	▬▬▬ 8.50 HUDDERSFIELD
50738	▬▬*8.49
50757	BLACKPOOL 6.51 ▬▬▬ 3.53 SOWERBY BRIDGE
50765	FLEETWOOD ▬▬▬ SOWERBY BRIDGE
50818	BOLTON 4.51 ▬▬▬ 5.52 LOW MOOR
50855	LOW MOOR ▬▬ 2.51 BOLTON
50859	BOLTON ▬▬▬▬▬*11.53

CLASS 0F 0-4-0ST

51222	▬▬▬▬ 2.50 GOOLE
51234	▬▬▬▬ 2.50 BANK HALL

CLASS 2F 0-6-0

51307	BANK HALL 2.57 ▬▬*11.57
51336	ROSE GROVE 8.54 ▬▬▬▬▬▬ 2.58 FLEETWOOD
51338	BURY ▬▬▬ 7.51 FLEETWOOD 9.51 ▪11.51 SOUTHPORT BURTON 2.57 ▬▬*8.57
51343	AINTREE 2.57 ▬▬▬▬▬*10.60
51358	BOLTON ▪ MIRFIELD

CLASS 2F 0-6-0 contd.

Page	No	
122	51371	BANK HALL 2.57 ▪ 3.57 BANK HALL ACCRINGTON 12.57 ▬▬▬ *3.61
	51379	▬▬▬ 2.50 GOOLE
	51381	SOWERBY BRIDGE 11.55 ▬▬▬ *11.57
	51390	ACCRINGTON 10.55 ▬▬ *7.56
	51400	▬▬ *10.49
	51404	▬▬▬ 2.50 LOW MOOR
122	51415	LOWER DARWEN 4.57 ▬▬▬ *10.58
	51424	▬▬▬ 1.50 MIRFIELD
	51425	▬▬▬▬▬▬ 8.53 SOUTHPORT
	51429	SOWERBY BRIDGE 5.50 ▬▬ 2.52 HORWICH WORKS
	51436	▬▬▬▬▬▬▬ *3.55
	51438	▬▬ *3.49
	51447	MIRFIELD 1.53 ▬▬▬▬▬ *1.57
	51457	WAKEFIELD 8.48 ▬▬▬▬▬▬▬▬▬ 9.57 LOSTOCK HALL 9.58 ▬▬ *3.59
122	51458	GOOLE 2.50 ▬▬▬▬▬▬▬▬ *5.59
	51470	▬▬▬▬▬▬ *10.55
	51472	▬▬▬▬▬▬ *4.55
	51481	BANK HALL 3.57 ▬▬ *11.57
	51488	SOWERBY BRIDGE 11.55 ▬▬ *3.56
	51496	▬▬▬▬▬▬ 5.57 AGECROFT
121	51497	ACCRINGTON 12.57 ▬▬ *5.59
	51510	▬▬▬▬▬ 7.51 BELLE VUE

Fowler Class 7F 0-8-0 No **49624**

L&Y Class 2P 2-4-2T No **50757**

L&Y Class 0F 0-4-0ST No **11234**

'A' CLASS 0-6-0

Page	No	
	52089	NORMANTON 1.53 ▬▬▬ 4.57 LOW MOOR
	52094	AINTREE 5.50 ▬▬▬ 5.53 BURY
	52102	BANK HALL ▬▬▬▬ 7.51 AGECROFT 9.51 ▬▬ *1.53
125	52108	LEES (OLDHAM) 2.53 ▬▬▬ 10.55 BOLTON 1.56 ▬▬ *10.59
	52120	▬▬▬ WAKEFIELD
	52124	▬▬▬ MIRFIELD
	52132	▬▬▬▬▬▬ 6.53 BOLTON
	52136	▬▬▬ BOLTON
	52137	AGECROFT ▬▬▬▬▬ *7.54
	52138	▬▬▬ BLACKPOOL
127	52139	BURY ▬▬▬ 10.52 BOLTON
	52140	SUTTON OAK 1.58 ▬▬▬ *6.60
	52141	NUNEATON 12.56 ▬▬▬▬ *5.60
	52156	▬▬▬▬▬ *2.53
	52159	BURY 1.53 ▬▬▬▬▬ *6.58
127	52161	HORWICH WORKS 3.58 ▬▬ *9.60
	52165	BURY 9.52 ▬▬▬▬▬ *4.57
	52207	▬▬▬▬ 6.53 BURY
	52219	▬▬▬ AGECROFT
	52229	▬▬ *8.49
123	52230	SPRINGS BRANCH (WIGAN) 5.58 ▬▬▬ *4.61
	52239	▬▬▬▬ 5.53 BURY
	52266	▬▬▬▬▬ *12.52
124	52270	BIRKENHEAD 2.57 ▬▬▬▬ *1.61
125·126	52271	BURY 5.53 ▬▬▬▬▬▬ 5.61 LEES (OLDHAM)
123-128	52275	WIGAN (L&Y) 12.56 ▬▬ 4.58 HORWICH WORKS 5.58 ▬▬▬ 8.60 LEES (OLDHAM)
	52278	AINTREE 11.56 ▬▬▬ *7.59
	52279	▬▬▬ AGECROFT
	52300	▬▬▬ 11.51 LOWER DARWEN 1.54 ▬▬ *1.56
	52304	AGECROFT 1.50 ▬▬▬ *1.53
	52317	LOSTOCK HALL 6.54 ▬▬ *5.55
	52322**	SUTTON OAK 1.58 ▬ 8.58 LEES (OLDHAM)
126	52328	BOLTON 1.54 ▬▬▬ *11.57
	52334	BOLTON 2.52 ▬▬▬ *12.54
128	52341	SPRINGS BRANCH (WIGAN) 12.56 ▬▬▬ *11.60
	52343	▬▬▬▬▬ 9.53 LOW MOOR
	52345	▬▬▬ WAKEFIELD
	52355	▬▬▬▬ 11.51 SOWERBY BRIDGE
	52358	▬▬▬▬ 7.51 AGECROFT 9.51 ▬▬▬ *12.56
	52360	LEES (OLDHAM) 4.53 ▬▬▬ 10.55 BOLTON

'A' CLASS 0-6-0 contd.

	52366	SUTTON OAK 1.58 � *4.58
	52389	LEES (OLDHAM) 2.52 ▬▬▬▬ 10.55 BOLTON
	52390	WIGAN (L&Y) 7.52 ▬▬▬ *8.56
126	**52431**	LOWER DARWEN 3.57 ▬▬▬▬▬ *12.59
	52437	▬▬ BLACKPOOL
	52443	▬▬ BACUP
	52455	BURY 5.50 ▬▬▬▬▬▬ *8.59
	52461	▬▬ LOW MOOR
	52466	▬▬ BLACKPOOL
	52517	▬▬▬▬▬ 4.53 CREWE WORKS
124	**52518**	▬▬ *2.49
	52558	BLACKPOOL ▬ 11.51 SOWERBY BRIDGE
	52569	LEES (OLDHAM) ▬ 6.53 LEES (OLDHAM)
	52578	▬▬ *2.49
	52581	▬▬ BURY
	52583	MIRFIELD ▬ *8.51

MIDLAND 2F 0-6-0

	58128	BELLE VUE 4.56 ▬ 4.57 BURTON

L&Y Class 2F 0-6-0ST No **51458**

L&Y Class 3F 0-6-0 No **52275**

Midland Class 2F 0-6-0 No **58128**

B1 CLASS 4-6-0

128	**61326**	GORTON 8.50 ▬ 9.50 GORTON

BRITANNIA CLASS 7P 4-6-2

129	**70000****	CREWE SOUTH 3.66 ▬ *5.66 *FOR PRESERVATION*
	70014	TRAFFORD PARK 12.60 ▬▬ 9.61 NEASDEN
	70015	TRAFFORD PARK 12.60 ▬▬ 9.61 NEASDEN
131	**70017**	CREWE SOUTH 7.65 ▬▬ 5.66 CARLISLE KINGMOOR
131	**70021**	CREWE SOUTH 7.65 ▬▬ 5.66 STOCKPORT EDGELEY
131	**70034**	CREWE SOUTH 7.65 ▬▬ 5.66 CARLISLE KINGMOOR
	70044	CREWE SOUTH 7.65 ▬▬ 5.66 STOCKPORT EDGELEY
130·132	**70045**	CAMDEN 1.60 ▬▬ 9.61 NEASDEN
129·130·132	**70048**	CAMDEN 1.60 ▬▬ 9.61 NEASDEN
	70049	CREWE NORTH 2.60 ▬▬ 9.61 NEASDEN

STANDARD CLASS 4 2-6-4T

134	**80044**	BURY 2.56 ▬▬▬▬ 3.60 CORKERHILL
	80046	BURY 2.56 ▬▬ 11.57 BLACKPOOL
	80049	NEW 11.52 ▬▬▬ 9.56 CHESTER
	80050	NEW 11.52 ▬▬▬ 9.56 CHESTER
	80051	NEW 11.52 ▬▬▬ 9.56 CHESTER
134	**80052**	NEW 12.52 ▬▬▬ 9.56 CHESTER
134	**80053**	NEW 12.52 ▬▬▬ 9.56 CHESTER
133	**80060**	BURY 2.56 ▬▬▬ 2.60 STIRLING
	80061	BURY 2.56 ▬▬▬ 3.60 STIRLING
133	**80093**	BURY 2.56 ▬▬ 11.57 BLACKPOOL

STANDARD CLASS 2 2-6-2T

	84025	BRIGHTON 9.61 ▬ 11.61 BOLTON
	84026	BRIGHTON 9.61 ▬ 10.61 BOLTON
	84027	BRIGHTON 9.61 ▬ 10.61 BOLTON
	84028	EASTLEIGH 9.61 ▬ 10.61 SKIPTON

BR Britannia Class 7P 4-6-2 No **70014**
Iron Duke

BR Class 4MT 2-6-4T No **80046**

WD Class 8F 2-8-0 No **90388**

PAGE 1948 ──▶ 1968

WD CLASS 8F 2-8-0

	90101	OLD OAK COMMON 12.50 ▦ 11.51 WAKEFIELD
141	**90105**	OLD OAK COMMON 12.50 ▦▦▦▦▦▦ *12.62
	90113	BIRKENHEAD 12.50 ▦▦▦▦▦ 11.57 SOWERBY BRIDGE
	90122	BELLE VUE 4.56 ▦ 10.56 SOWERBY BRIDGE
	90123	SHREWSBURY 12.50 ▦ 12.51 BURY
	90126	BELLE VUE 4.56 ▦ 10.56 LOW MOOR
	90140	BELLE VUE 4.56 ▦▦ 11.57 LEES (OLDHAM)
	90142	BELLE VUE 4.56 ▦▦▦▦▦ 5.61 AGECROFT
	90155	EX-WR 12.50 ▦ 12.50 STOCKTON
138	**90163**	BELLE VUE 4.56 ▦▦▦▦▦▦ *12.62
	90173	SWANSEA VICTORIA 1.51 ▦▦▦ 10.53 BIRKENHEAD
	90183	PATRICROFT 1.63 ▦ 12.63 SPRINGS BRANCH
	90197	BELLE VUE 4.56 ▦▦▦▦▦ *5.64
	90219	GRANGEMOUTH 8.51 ▦▦ 3.53 BURY
142	**90222**	EASTFIELD 8.51 ▦▦▦▦ 2.60 PATRICROFT
	90226	BRICKLAYER'S ARMS 4.51 ▦ 9.51 SOWERBY BRIDGE 10.51 ▦▦ 11.53 BURY
	90245	FARNLEY JUNCTION 5.51 ▦▦▦ 12.59 AINTREE
138	**90248**	ST. MARGARETS 8.51 ▦▦▦▦▦ 9.62 PATRICROFT 1.63 ▦ 3.64 BOLTON
	90265	EASTFIELD 8.51 ▦ 9.51 WAKEFIELD
	90271	LEES (OLDHAM) 5.58 ▦▦▦▦▦ 7.64 AINTREE
	90283	ROSE GROVE 11.53 ▦▦ 7.56 AINTREE
136·142	**90289**	ST. MARGARETS 8.51 ▦▦▦▦ 6.58 LANCASTER 9.58 ▦▦ 7.64 AINTREE
136	**90291**	ST. MARGARETS 8.51 ▦▦▦▦▦ 7.64 ROSE GROVE
	90316	BELLE VUE 4.56 ▦▦▦ 6.58 LANCASTER
	90327	SHREWSBURY 12.50 ▦▦ 6.58 LANCASTER
139	**90328**	LOSTOCK HALL 1.59 ▦▦ 9.62 PATRICROFT 1.63 ▦ *5.64
	90331	PATRICROFT 2.63 ▦ *11.63
	90338	8.50 ▦▦▦▦▦ *11.63
	90346	WOODFORD HALSE 4.64 ▦ 6.64 AINTREE
	90360	REDHILL 7.51 ▦▦▦ 7.56 SOWERBY BRIDGE
140	**90366**	SHREWSBURY 12.50 ▦▦▦▦▦ *1.64
	90371	PATRICROFT 1.63 ▦▦ *4.64
142	**90376**	ST. MARGARETS 8.51 ▦▦▦▦ *12.62
	90379	8.50 WAKEFIELD
140	**90388**	8.50 ▦▦▦▦▦▦ 7.64 ROSE GROVE
	90389	HITHER GREEN 8.51 ▦▦▦▦▦ 7.64 ROSE GROVE
136·140·141	**90390**	HITHER GREEN 4.51 ▦▦▦▦▦ 9.62 PATRICROFT 1.63 ▦ 1.64 GORTON
	90398	AINTREE 6.51 ▦ 10.51 SOWERBY BRIDGE LEES (OLDHAM) 4.64 ▦ 7.64 LOWER DARWEN
	90413	SHREWSBURY 12.50 ▦▦ 12.51 BURY
	90516	WOODFORD HALSE 4.64 ▦▦ 9.64 AINTREE
	90520	WOODFORD HALSE 4.64 ▦ 6.64 AINTREE 8.64 ▦ 9.64 AINTREE
137	**90523**	PERTH 8.51 ▦▦▦▦ *12.62
	90525	11.49 ▦▦▦▦ 6.58 LEES (OLDHAM) 4.64 ▦ *5.64
137	**90530**	PERTH 8.51 ▦▦▦ 2.60 PATRICROFT 1.63 ▦ *5.63
	90533	BRICKLAYER'S ARMS 7.51 ▦▦▦▦▦ 2.64 AGECROFT
	90535	BIRKENHEAD 12.50 ▦▦ 11.55 AINTREE
	90548	SHREWSBURY 12.50 ▦▦▦▦ 4.62 PATRICROFT 1.63 ▦ *5.64
	90552	BRICKLAYER'S ARMS 8.51 ▦ 2.52 BELLE VUE 3.56 ▦▦ 11.58 AINTREE
	90558	BRICKLAYER'S ARMS 7.51 ▦▦▦ 11.58 AGECROFT
135·141	**90561**	SHREWSBURY 12.50 ▦▦▦ 1.59 WIGAN (L&Y) 2.60 ▦▦▦ 7.64 AINTREE
135	**90568**	SWANSEA VICTORIA 12.50 ▦▦ 11.53 BURY PATRICROFT 1.63 ▦ *1.64
	90576	ROSE GROVE 11.53 ▦▦▦ 4.60 AINTREE
	90584	WIGAN (L&Y) 2.58 ▦ 6.58 HELLIFIELD
	90589	SHREWSBURY 12.50 ▦▦▦ 9.57 AGECROFT LEES (OLDHAM) 5.58 ▦ 4.62 PATRICROFT
	90641	REDHILL 7.51 ▦ 4.53 BOLTON
138	**90669**	HITHER GREEN 6.51 ▦▦▦▦ 1.60 PATRICROFT
	90675	PERTH 8.51 ▦▦ 11.55 AINTREE 2.58 ▦ 2.59 LOSTOCK HALL
	90697	WOODFORD HALSE 4.64 ▦ 8.64 SPRINGS BRANCH
	90706	11.49 ▦▦▦▦ 6.58 HELLIFIELD
	90708	11.49 ▦ 9.51 MOLD JUNCTION LEES (OLDHAM) 4.64 ▦ *5.64
139	**90715**	SHREWSBURY 12.50 ▦▦▦▦▦ *5.64
	90718	LEES (OLDHAM) 4.64 ▦ 9.64 AINTREE

CLASS 9F 2-10-0

	92010	LEICESTER (MIDLAND) 3.64 ▬ 6.64 CARLISLE KINGMOOR
144	92015	SALTLEY 6.58 ▬▬ 9.62 BOLTON 12.62 ▬▬▬▬ 6.67 CARLISLE KINGMOOR
143·149	92016	SALTLEY 6.58 ▬▬ 9.62 BOLTON 12.62 ▬▬▬▬ 6.67 CARNFORTH
144·146	92017	SALTLEY 6.58 ▬▬ 9.62 BOLTON 12.62 ▬▬ 6.64 CARLISLE KINGMOOR
	92018	KIRKBY IN ASHFIELD 9.64 ▬▬ 8.66 CARLISLE KINGMOOR
143·146	92022	TOTON 6.64 ▬▬ 2.66 SPEKE JUNCTION
	92026	KIRKBY IN ASHFIELD 9.64 ▬ 5.65 BIRKENHEAD
	92031	WESTHOUSES 7.65 ▬ *1.67
	92050	KIRKBY IN ASHFIELD 10.64 ▬ 2.66 SPEKE JUNCTION
	92051	KIRKBY IN ASHFIELD 10.64 ▬ 11.65 CARLISLE KINGMOOR
	92052	KIRKBY IN ASHFIELD 10.64 ▬▬ 6.67 CARLISLE KINGMOOR
	92056	KIRKBY IN ASHFIELD 10.64 ▬ 8.66 CARLISLE KINGMOOR
	92071	ANNESLEY 7.65 ▬ 12.65 CARLISLE KINGMOOR
	92076	KIRKBY IN ASHFIELD 10.64 ▬ 1.65 CARLISLE KINGMOOR
145·148	92077	KIRKBY IN ASHFIELD 6.64 ▬▬▬ 3.67 CARNFORTH
145·146	92080	KETTERING 6.64 ▬▬ 8.66 CARLISLE KINGMOOR
	92081	KETTERING 6.64 ▬▬ *2.66
	92110	KIRKBY IN ASHFIELD 9.64 ▬ 5.65 CARLISLE KINGMOOR
	92114	KIRKBY IN ASHFIELD 9.64 ▬ 5.65 CARLISLE KINGMOOR
	92159	KIRKBY IN ASHFIELD 9.64 ▬ 5.65 BIRKENHEAD
144·147·149	92161	WESTHOUSES 6.58 ▬▬▬▬▬▬ 5.65 CARLISLE KINGMOOR
146·147	92162	WESTHOUSES 6.58 ▬▬▬▬▬▬ 5.65 BIRKENHEAD
148	92208	CARDIFF EAST DOCK 10.63 ▬ 6.64 CARLISLE KINGMOOR
	92233	NEWPORT EBBW JUNCTION 10.63 ▬ 6.64 CARLISLE KINGMOOR
148	92247	BANBURY 9.66 ▬ *10.66
	92249	NEWPORT EBBW JUNCTION 10.63 ▬ 6.64 CARLISLE KINGMOOR

Standard 9F 2-10-0 No 92017 descending towards Stansfield Hall, approaching Knotts Road overbridge. **28TH DECEMBER 1962** ● R.S. GREENWOOD

NEWTON HEATH ENGINES AT WORK
1948 -1968

FRONT COVER. **Newton Heath's great diversity of motive power** during the BR period was represented by 29 different classes of locomotive. The Hughes/Fowler 2-6-0 'Crabs' were one of the the most popular, being able to cope with a wide range of duties and the lined livery of No **42789** is seen to good effect high in the Pennine hills whilst working a mixed freight near Marsden. Along with Nos 42713 and 42766, the loco moved on to Farnley Junction in May 1956. **10TH OCTOBER 1953** ● B.K.B. GREEN

BACK COVER. **Jubilee** 4-6-0 No **45654** *Hood.*
Manchester Victoria Station. **1966** ● AUTHOR'S COLLECTION

Class Five 4-6-0 Nos **44890** and **44891**.
York. **20th MARCH 1948** ● G. COLTAS

'A' Class 0-6-0 No **52431**.
Manchester Victoria Station. **1957** ● AUTHOR'S COLLECTION

Jinty 0-6-0 No **47408**.
Newton Heath. **1964** ● J. DAVENPORT

Standard 9F 2-10-0 No **92017**.
Castleton. **18TH JUNE 1960** ● R.S. GREENWOOD

Fairburn 2-6-4T No **42284**.
Middleton Station. **22ND JULY 1952** ● H.D. BOWTELL

Fowler 0-8-0 No **49508**.
Manchester Victoria Station. **17TH AUGUST 1960** ● M.S. STOKES

Fowler 0-6-0 No **44022**.
Royton Junction. **30TH APRIL 1960** ● P. HUTCHINSON

Steam IMAGE